MESSAGES

MESSAGES

Signs, Visits, and Premonitions
from Loved Ones Lost on 9/11

BONNIE
McENEANEY

WILLIAM MORROW *An Imprint of* HarperCollinsPublishers

MESSAGES. Copyright © 2010 by Bonnie McEneaney. All rights reserved. Printed in the United States of America. No part of this book may be used or reproduced in any manner whatsoever without written permission except in the case of brief quotations embodied in critical articles and reviews. For information address Harper-Collins Publishers, 10 East 53rd Street, New York, NY 10022.

HarperCollins books may be purchased for educational, business, or sales promotional use. For information please write: Special Markets Department, Harper-Collins Publishers, 10 East 53rd Street, New York, NY 10022.

FIRST EDITION

Designed by Joy O'Meara

Library of Congress Cataloging-in-Publication Data has been applied for.

ISBN 978-0-06-197407-6

10 11 12 13 14   OV/RRD   10 9 8 7 6 5 4 3

For Susan, Laurie, Blayney, Patrick, Kevin, and Maureen—
I dedicate this book to you

Faith is to believe what you do not see;
the reward of this faith is to see what you believe.

— Saint Augustine

CONTENTS

Introduction   I

PART ONE: THE JOURNEY BEGINS

Chapter One: My Story   9

PART TWO: THE UNBROKEN CONNECTION

Chapter Two: I'm Here . . . I'm Okay . . . I Love You   39

Chapter Three: Going Forward with Love   61

Chapter Four: Many Messages, Much Inspiration   87

Chapter Five: Finding a More Spiritual Perspective   105

PART THREE: GLIMPSES OF A DEEPER REALITY

Chapter Six: Premonitions: Warnings from the Universe?   119

Chapter Seven: Signs of Spiritual Connection   153

Chapter Eight: Dreams and Visitations   181

Chapter Nine: Mediums: When Others Hear the Message   199

PART FOUR: THE MESSAGE IS LOVE

Chapter Ten: Love is Forever   223

Afterword   247

"A Bend in the Road" by Eamon J. McEneaney   251

Acknowledgments   253

MESSAGES

INTRODUCTION

This is a book about men and women who lost loved ones and who have been fortunate enough to have spiritual experiences surrounding these losses. This is *not* a book about death. It is a book about hope and the deep and loving connections that go well beyond the boundaries that exist between life and death.

After my husband, Eamon McEneaney, died in the World Trade Center, I was almost immediately in touch with other 9/11 family members. Within days I started hearing about their spiritual experiences and, in fact, began to have some of my own. I'd like to say that even the most subtle of my experiences have touched me greatly and helped me through my own healing process. They have given me a firm sense that the spirit never truly dies and that our spiritual connection with those we love is never lost. Most of the people who are certain they have known after-death communication say these experiences have given them comfort and peace. Mine have done the same for me. Part of the purpose of this book is to share these feelings with readers who are struggling with loss and may also need assurance and comfort.

Accepting the finality of death has always presented a challenge to the human psyche. Nothing can change it. It just "is." Anyone who has experienced a loss knows what it feels like. Time and time again, we ask ourselves the following questions: "Where did he go?" "What happened to her?" "How could this be?" When a loved one dies, communication is terminated forever. This is a difficult concept for us to process and believe. But what if this isn't the case? What if communication doesn't end, but simply is transformed? What if we discovered that most, if not all, of the people who have left our earthly existence have sent their loved ones messages—messages that we have overlooked because of our own limited human understanding. What if they regularly send signs that we miss because we don't know how to interpret the evidence? What if they are trying to communicate with us, and we're just not paying attention? Why is this possibility such a difficult one to grasp?

Many of us belong to organized religions in which we are taught to believe in a higher power—a God or Supreme Being. We are told that there is "more" than this earthly life we lead—whether heaven, nirvana, or any other ecclesiastical representation of what this "more" might be. But, ironically, even though we are taught religious doctrines from the time we are children, regularly participating in spiritually based practices in various houses of worship and even at home, when there's a possible sign that, indeed, there is "more," we tend to remain either doubtful and unconvinced or embarrassed that others will think we are somehow gullible or foolish. We still remain a society that requires "proof" to believe in anything unconventional. And what defines "proof" anyway, when it comes to the spiritual world? What has to occur to transform a skeptic into a believer?

In the summer of 2001, my husband was positive that his death was imminent and communicated a series of compelling premonitions, including a discussion on how to escape from the Trade Center in the event of the attack he was sure was coming. This particular exchange took place on the Sunday of Labor Day weekend, nine days before September 11th, and precipitated a week filled with numerous other disturbing comments from Eamon relating to the imminence of his death—and that he "could handle it now."

After my husband's death, I couldn't help but think about his various heartfelt statements and what his words meant. I was also starting to have an overwhelming awareness of his presence along with the sense that he was somehow trying to communicate and send me signs that he was "okay." I was having a difficult time understanding what was happening to me. Was this simply a manifestation of grief? I eventually began to ask others who had lost loved ones on 9/11 if they, too, had encountered anything similar. I was amazed at the responses. Many said that either they or their deceased loved ones had shared strong premonitions. Many also told me about powerful occurrences in their own lives that led them to believe that their loved ones were trying to send messages or signs that were impossible to ignore. Most told me that they had a unique and visceral sense of their loved one's presence guiding them and giving them strength. An astonishing number told me that either they or other family members had actually seen their loved one's spirit.

Several of the people who strongly believed that they were getting messages from their deceased loved ones were reluctant to broadcast their experiences. Respected members of their communities, they didn't want others to think that they were delusional. I was not surprised by these feelings and totally understood how they felt. At the time, although I considered myself a spiritual person, I was also more than a little bit skeptical about the possibility of other dimensions or discovering that there was "more" after this lifetime; I also tended to view people who had strong beliefs in the "paranormal" as being a bit "off" or "different." I had no experiences that helped me relate to their thinking. After all, I was a business executive—not the kind of person who tried to solve problems by consulting psychics or mediums.

Nonetheless, as my discussions with others continued, I was extremely motivated to do more personal exploration into what was going on. As I've pressed forward, I've been quite taken aback by what I've observed in my own life. As a result of my own experiences, combined with all the interviews I've completed, I can no longer question the existence of a spiritual, perhaps divine, component to all of this that defies human logic. The widespread premonitions described by victims before the terrorist attacks are very compelling. What some

9/11 family members have experienced after the attacks may be even more so. These people have told me that they have seen and felt things that they can neither ignore nor explain and that they now approach the world with an enhanced spiritual perspective. As this book was getting ready to go into production, I was shown an amazing photograph of a little girl named Alexis sitting in a field with a beam of light radiating down on her. Her father, Rick Thorpe, perished in the South Tower of the World Trade Center. Her mother, Linda, took the photograph in the summer of 2002. They were in Ireland for a family wedding.

"It was a cloudy Irish day," Linda told me, "and my daughter just walked out to this open grassy area by the church and plopped down. It was very unlike her to do something like that, which is why I took the picture. When she walked out like that, I thought, 'What is she doing?' She looked like an angel, but I saw no beam of light." When Linda got the picture back, she couldn't explain the beam of light. Her father-in-law took the picture and the camera to an expert who assured him that there was nothing wrong with the camera or the film.

Linda was originally very skeptical and disbelieving of the possibility of continued spiritual connection, but this photograph, along with

Alexis in a field in Shannon, Ireland

other signs that cannot be explained, has altered her perspective. "Initially I thought, 'This is weird,'" Linda said. "Now I know they are out there. It's magical. Alexis's daddy was at the wedding. He will always be watching out for her and me."

The men and women who lost loved ones on 9/11 represent a cross section of American life. Their many spiritual experiences deserve broader exploration. Of course, it stands to reason that people practicing an organized religion, professing an afterlife, will have the desire— the yearning—to believe, even if they are skeptical. The experiences in *Messages* collectively suggest the potential existence of "more" than this life—that there might really be "another side." They are important because they arguably serve as some level of evidence that death is the precursor of the transformation of the soul, and our relationships continue. Clearly this is quite a provocative concept, but it's one that has existed (and has been repeatedly challenged) since the beginning of time.

Most people have read or heard about what outstanding individuals the victims of 9/11 were. It's fitting that the miraculous stories that fill the pages of *Messages* will help to preserve their legacy. I truly believe that the combined experiences of so many people who are receiving these messages will help all of us open our eyes to a universe of new spiritual possibility.

Surely, all the inexplicable stories surrounding 9/11 can't be explained away by the word "coincidence." Many have spoken of having a sense that greater wisdom from another realm of existence has been pointing a finger and saying: Notice this. Fate is winking. Pay attention. Something is going on here, something that can't be explained. It shouldn't be ignored and deserves greater examination.

PART ONE

THE JOURNEY BEGINS

In the hours and days that immediately followed the destruction of the World Trade Center, I had no idea what had happened to my husband. Victims' family members were given very little information and, in some instances, were even encouraged to believe our loved ones had survived and were somehow lost, in hospital burn units, wandering the streets of New York City or, worse, lying in the smoldering rubble that came to be known as the pile. That's why so many of us were posting signs throughout the city. My sister-in-law Debbie had gone to the New York armory to fill out a missing persons report. I was so thankful for her help. She tacked Eamon's picture under the sign that read **MISSING. HAVE YOU SEEN THESE PEOPLE?** We were waiting and hoping.

Eamon McEneaney on the
Missing Persons Wall

CHAPTER ONE

My Story

It must have been two or three days after September 11th when I had the first inkling that communication doesn't always end with death. Our house in Connecticut was buzzing with people—friends, neighbors, and relatives, some of them on cell phones still calling burn units and emergency rooms. The television, fixed on a news channel, was going constantly. The halls were lined with flower arrangements, and the counters and refrigerator were overflowing with food—fruit, beverages, casseroles, salads, and desserts—generously brought or sent by so many people whose kindness I will never forget.

I remember stepping out of our front door. It was an incredibly beautiful and still morning, and as I looked around, I couldn't help but be aware of how much of my husband Eamon was present around me. Our backyard is surrounded by a low stone wall. It looks as if it might have been built by early settlers, but in truth my husband had constructed it himself, stone by stone, using the boulders that he found—some from the decaying walls that were lying haphazardly on our property, others that he'd dug from deep in the earth. Every time I look at it, I remember how hard Eamon worked. The garden in the backyard is also filled with lush red rosebushes, planted and carefully tended by Eamon. About thirty yards from our house, overlooking the area where the children played, is a tree on which he had carved LOVE IS FOREVER. As I looked around, Eamon was everywhere, but he wasn't there. Where was he?

Standing outside the door, surrounded by the still, green trees, I didn't know what to think, and I didn't know what to do. It didn't seem possible that my larger-than-life husband could have disappeared off the face of the earth; it didn't seem possible that he could be dead. Then, without thinking about it, I spontaneously opened my mouth and I yelled, "Eamon, where are you???" When I heard the words, it was almost as if it was somebody else's voice—as though I had no control over what was coming out of my mouth. I wanted my husband to answer. I wanted him to tell me where he was, but I also recognized I was making an impossible request.

Everything around me was still—not a ripple in the air. Then, all of sudden, somewhere above me, I heard the beginning rush of a gust of new wind building up in intensity. The sound grew louder. I looked above the trees—the tall oak, maple, and black birch that frame the entrance to my driveway, and I could see the wind! It created such a strong pattern through the leaves and the trees that it was easy to follow. It had the outline of a river, undulating across and around, swirling and turning as it made its way toward me. I stared, dumbstruck. This river of wind had a life of its own. I watched as it whimsically played with my skirt, lifting it up and gently letting it fall. Then, just as suddenly as it started, it stopped . . . cold . . . just like that. No sound. No breeze. The air was still. It didn't seem possible, yet I knew that I had asked, "Eamon, where are you?" And I knew my question had been answered. I didn't have a bit of doubt about the truth of what I had experienced. "He's gone," I thought. "It's over."

I didn't know how to explain the river of wind I had just seen and felt. I had no firm information about where it had come from or what had caused it, and yet I knew absolutely it was connected to Eamon and that the sad message it brought was true and real. I stood there for a moment in my quiet yard before walking back into the house and telling everyone what I had witnessed. Nobody questioned either my experience or my interpretation. I remember people looking at me with astonished eyes. No one spoke. We all knew Eamon was gone. Later, I remembered something my completely down-to-earth father had shocked me by saying. On two separate occasions before his own death in 1993, my father had promised, "You know, Bonnie, when I die, I'll speak to you through the wind." Eamon had done just that.

Over the years I had heard various people talk about receiving "signs" that were either mystical in nature or that they interpreted as messages from the dead. Personally, however, until the day I saw that river of wind, I'd had no spiritual experiences like this and was more than a little bit skeptical about the possibility of communication with another dimension. But in the months and years after 9/11, I would learn more about the various ways in which people describe contact with those who have passed over.

When a loved one dies, many, for example, say that they become more aware of being surrounded by spiritual energy. I've spoken to a man who told me of holding two separate individuals when they died and feeling a sensation not unlike energy passing from their bodies through his own. Others describe hearing a *whoosh* sensation or sound. As I've interviewed people for this book, I've heard this descriptive word, *whoosh,* used often.

Vicki Davis, an Episcopal priest in Connecticut where I live, told me about returning home from the funeral of her thirtysomething-year-old sister and falling asleep exhausted. Vicki, who at that time was still in a seminary, woke up startled by a bright light in the hallway outside her bedroom. At first she was apprehensive and a little frightened because she was positive that she had turned the light out; she also didn't understand how she could have fallen asleep with so much light. When she stepped out of her bedroom into the hall, she walked into the light and realized that it was coming from a source much more intense than the overhead fixture. She said that she didn't know how long she stayed there, surrounded by light, but she knew that it was connected to her sister, and that it was her sister's way of communicating that she was okay. She told me that she was awestruck and completely grateful for what had happened because it brought her a great feeling of peace and comfort. When the light left, she heard a *whoosh*. Later, several times in her ministerial work, when she was present with people who were dying, she also experienced the same kind of *whoosh*, which she could only interpret as coming from the spirit leaving the body.

It is also very common for men and women to say they have dreams of being visited by the spirits of loved ones who have died; sometimes these loved ones even convey special messages. One of my neighbors, for example, told me that after his father died, he was unable to locate some papers that were important to the estate. He had just about given up his search when he had a dream in which his father came and gave him precise instructions on where to locate the missing documents.

When people have experiences like this, they are frequently reluctant to talk about them because they don't want others to think they are being illogical or "weird," for want of a better word. It was only after I began to do research for this book that my mother surprised me by telling me, in a matter-of-fact tone, that her mother (my grandmother) had seen her own mother after she died. My mother remembers my grandmother being absolutely positive about what she saw. Yet my mother wasn't comfortable about sharing any of this until I introduced the subject of after-death communication. "There's something I never told you before," she confessed. "What do you think about all this?" I asked my mother. "I don't know what to think," she replied.

In the time period that surrounds a loved one's death, we often experience events that appear difficult to understand. It's not unusual for some people to talk about photos that seem to jump off of shelves or walls and fall to the floor; others speak about finding coins with significant dates in unusual locations; many have dramatic experiences with birds or butterflies. Some of us are immediately certain that these occurrences are "signs" or "messages" and should be regarded as such, while others shrug them off as mere coincidence, even when the events seem to defy the odds.

My friend Julie, for example, recently told me the following story concerning her mother, Helen, who died about a year ago. Julie's five-year-old grandson Alex* was visiting for a few weeks in the summer. In previous years, Julie's mother would have been visiting as well, because she adored Alex and loved to spend time with him. Julie was sitting in her home office, and Alex was running up and down the hall outside her door. Julie's once-a-week cleaning woman, Joan, was playing with Alex. Every time Alex raced by the door, Joan would reach out and grab the boy, saying, "I'm going to give you a speeding ticket." Alex would crack up, laughing so hard that he would practically fall to the floor before he started running again.

As Julie looked at what was happening, she thought of her mother, who despite her age had played with her great-grandchildren in a very physical way. "If my mother were here," Julie thought, "this is exactly how she would be playing with Alex." At that moment, Joan turned away from the hall and came back into Julie's office.

"I just vacuumed in here," Joan said. "Where did this come from?"

She pointed to what looked like a piece of paper on the floor. When Joan turned it over, and held it up, they could see that it was a photograph of Julie's mother that minutes before had been in a frame on the back of a bookshelf. How did that get there? Julie wondered. How did it get out of the frame and how did it get on the floor? And why at this precise moment? Thinking about all the circumstances of the photo on the floor, Julie said that she could come to no other conclusion than that her mother somehow was enjoying watching Alex playing and trying to send a message that she was there in spirit.

From my research and experiences after my husband's death, I have learned more about what one can expect in terms of signs. In my own life, there are moments when something happens that is so unusual that I am positive it is a sign; other times I'm not so sure.

There must have been two thousand people who came to Eamon's memorial service. Cornell, my husband's alma mater, sent the lacrosse team and the football team, as well as the Glee Club. Friends and family from across the country and the world arrived to pay their respects.

At the service, people commented on several happenings. The first revolved around Eamon's oldest brother, Blayney, a Vietnam veteran, high school teacher, lacrosse coach, and mentor to many. Blayney ended his eulogy to his brother by reading Tennyson's poem "Ring Out, Wild Bells." The poem begins:

Ring out, wild bells, to the wild sky,
The flying cloud, the frosty light:
The year is dying in the night;
Ring out, wild bells, and let him die.

Ring out the old, ring in the new,
Ring happy bells, across the snow:
The year is going, let him go;
Ring out the false, ring in the true.

One of the stanzas in the middle of the poem reads,

Ring out false pride in place and blood,
The civic slander and the spite;
Ring in the love of truth and right,
Ring in the common love of good.

Suddenly, as Blayney spoke the words *Ring in the love of truth and right*, the clock struck twelve, and church bells throughout the town began to chime wildly in the background. For a minute there, it seemed as though every church in our Connecticut town was joining in. Was this a "sign" or was it coincidence? As dramatic as it was at the time, it makes sense to chalk this up as coincidence. My brother-in-law started reading the poem at exactly the time when local churches often ring their bells. But then, another strange event happened during the service.

My husband had been exceptionally close to many of the men with whom he worked. Like Eamon, they were also killed on 9/11. The widows of two of these men, Joanne and Eileen, were sitting in the middle of the church. After the service they came up to tell me that something unusual had occurred: As they sat in their pew, a thin white powdery substance began to fall on both of them. When they looked up, they couldn't see it coming down or anything on the ceiling that could have caused it. They were also taken aback to realize that they were the only people in the entire church to whom this had happened. Nothing had fallen on anybody else around them. A mutual friend sitting behind them noticed it as well. "What is that stuff!?" he whispered, leaning forward in his seat. "And why is it only falling on you?" Was this a coincidence, or was it a sign? To be perfectly honest, I have no idea. What I do know is that after the service, the three of us stood together outside the church, all deeply in mourning, and all feeling that somehow our husbands were there with us, comforting us and telling us to be strong.

Mingled with my grief after 9/11 was a strong sense of disbelief. How was it possible that my incredibly athletic and charismatic husband had died? How could it be that we would no longer be together? Eamon and I had met twenty-five years earlier in the fall of 1976. We were both students at Cornell. He was a legend in the world of lacrosse; everyone who followed the sport knew about Eamon. Huge crowds would come to games simply to see him perform his magical ballet on the field. Eamon loved everything about lacrosse! He was so respectful of the Native American origins of the game that he continued to play with a wooden stick long after wood had been abandoned in favor of plastic or metal. He loved his stick's worn appearance, with the cat gut pocket that he spent hours repairing. In an article that he wrote for *Lacrosse Magazine* many years after we met, he said:

The beauty of this ancient crosier is not its perfection, but rather its imperfection. They say that players' skills have improved and are much superior to those of the players of the past, and perhaps they have. But when I look at the great game of my childhood and I dream of the ancient fathers and the great spirits of the game of lacrosse, I see them barefoot, in buckskin, on fields that stretch as far as the eye can see—and they're cradling their imperfect sticks.

It was Eamon's battered wooden stick that helped him break the record for the most points in an NCAA lacrosse championship tournament, a record he still holds, tied in 1987 by another Cornellian, Tim Goldstein. One wonders what other records he might have held if he had had stats for four seasons instead of three, if he hadn't been taken out of some of the games when the point spread became too wide, and if he had played with a modern stick.

I talked to his legendary coach and good friend, Richie Moran. "To this day, there has never been a player who could pass and assist like he did," Richie told me. "He was the most dynamic person to ever play the game—the most gifted athlete I've ever worked with. He led by example. He had so much love for his teammates. He could have been sensational at any sport and he did so much for lacrosse—because of his energy, his endurance, his tenacity, his hard work." At the end of our discussion, Richie told me that his son, Kevin, had named his son Eamon—something I never knew.

Eamon's skill and his love of the game combined to make him unstoppable; he would weave his way through the players on the opposing team and score so quickly that they didn't even know what had happened. It was only fitting that in 1993, Eamon was inducted into the Lacrosse Hall of Fame.

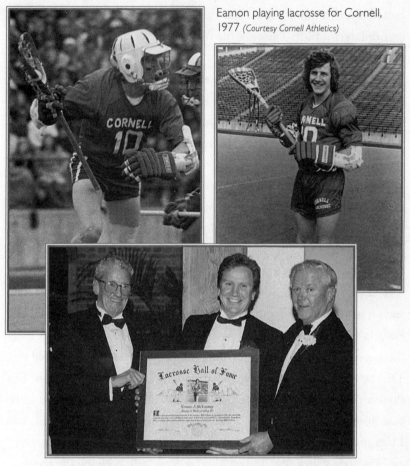

Eamon playing lacrosse for Cornell, 1977 *(Courtesy Cornell Athletics)*

Eamon *(center)* at his induction into the Lacrosse Hall of Fame with his father, Ed McEneaney *(left)* and his coach and good friend, Richie Moran *(Courtesy US Lacrosse)*

In 1976, I was a new student on the Cornell campus, but even I had heard about Eamon. One evening my roommate, Kathy, and I decided to visit a popular bar in the area called "The Nines." I had actually noticed Eamon's picture in a football program earlier in the day (he was also an all-American wide receiver) and had told Kathy that I wanted to meet him.

When Eamon entered the bar, he was with a bunch of his team-mates, and they were all wearing towels. Considering that they had just finished a streaking rally on campus, the towels were clearly better than the alternative. He came and stood at the bar near me and ordered a beer. I wanted to start a conversation. "Nice outfit," I remarked.

Eamon and I didn't really date at Cornell, but we became good friends. I remember that the first time we spent an evening together, we had enough money between us for two movie tickets to *Saturday Night Fever* and one sandwich. Even though it was apparent that there was something special about our relationship, it didn't really take off until years later when we met again at a party in New York City in August 1982. Many things impressed me about Eamon, including his deep devotion to his family and friends and his sense of humor.

I recently spoke to one of his closest friends from childhood, Ron Spottz. "I don't remember not knowing Eamon," Ron explained. "He was always fiercely loyal to his friends. Unbelievably so! And he had such a genius for competition. I'll never forget when I was eleven, and he was ten, we had a field day. I was a sprinter, and he was a long-distance runner. He talked me into running the mile. Eamon told me, 'On the second half of the last lap, you're not going to want to run. Just don't let the other guys know that because they're all feeling the same way. Just keep going.' Because of his coaching, I came in second, and I had no right."

Anybody who knew Eamon also couldn't help noticing the compassion he felt for those in need. Richie Moran remembers walking with Eamon through the streets of New York City. "Hello, Eamon," said a voice. Richie realized it came from a disheveled-looking homeless man sitting on the sidewalk, leaning against the wall of a building.

"Hey, Tom, how ya doin'?" Eamon replied cheerfully.

Richie, astonished, looked at Eamon. "How do you know him?" he asked.

"I take him to lunch now and then" was Eamon's response.

Eamon and I married in 1986, had four wonderful children together, and eventually moved from New York to Connecticut. By 2001, my husband had been working at Cantor Fitzgerald for ten years in the area of mortgage-backed securities. He loved the guys he worked with, but he hated the commute and the extreme stress of the job. Even though it wasn't realistic, we had talked often about finding ways for him to cut back. Eamon was a wonderful and talented writer. We both wanted him to have the chance to do what he wanted to do— work on the books and poems he was carrying around in his head.

Like many people who lose loved ones, no matter what the circumstances, I couldn't help but focus on all the what-ifs. The morning of 9/11, Eamon had an attack of vertigo, something that hadn't happened for almost a year. I wanted him to stay home. Later, I would ask myself: Why did he have vertigo on that particular day? Why was he so determined to go to work? What if I had been able to convince him to stay home or go in later? What if I had somehow been able to force him to quit his job after the '93 bombing? What-if scenarios kept running through my brain. In my case, these thoughts were particularly loud because of the many premonitions Eamon had shared with me and other family members.

In the weeks and days immediately preceding the attacks on the World Trade Center, my husband appeared to have a sense that something monumental was imminent. Let me start by saying that he always believed he would die young and carried with him an awareness of the fleeting nature of life. Not only was Eamon a world-class athlete, but he was also a wonderful writer, a poet who could spin pictures with words. When he came home from work, he would often disappear behind closed doors in the den to listen to music and to write. Reading his poetry now, one can't help but notice how much of it deals with death. This was as true of what he wrote when he was in his teens as it was of his writing from 2001. Back in the 1980s, when he was still in his twenties, he dedicated a poem to his family. In part, it reads:

> *The family grows old and dusty,*
>   *death lurks at each corner of our lives.*

The clock on my wall smiles,
  it is patient.
I bless the fractional moment on earth that we
  have touched together.
If nothing more,
  you,
my family,
  have made me love.

Eamon and his siblings *(left to right)*: Patrick, Susan, Blayney, Laurie, Eamon, Kevin, and Maureen

Throughout our years together, every now and then Eamon would throw out random predictions about the future. He always predicted that he would not survive the millennium. As the year 2000 approached, Eamon reminded me time and again that the millennium began in January of 2001, not 2000, and that not only was he going to die, but that the world as we knew it was going to end. However, even though he talked about a hit on the World Trade Center, I don't believe he necessarily associated his death with an event in the towers. Perhaps he didn't know how he was going to die, but in hindsight, there is no question in my mind that he knew his death was looming on the horizon.

By late August 2001, Eamon, more restless and distracted than I had ever before seen him, was making dire predictions about his fate almost daily. Ron Spottz told me: "The first time Eamon ever said anything strange to me was in July 2001. We were playing golf on the Captain's Course on Cape Cod. I remember it like it was yesterday, and I still think about what he said. Eamon was about ten feet ahead of me, walking down an incline, and he turned and said, 'Spotty, let me tell you. Bin Laden's the one who's going to do us in. You have to do things now in your life and not wait—you never know when your number's up.' To be perfectly honest, I thought he was being ridiculous, and I said, 'Come on, Mac, he's just some guy living in a cave. . . .' And Eamon said, 'A cave, my ass . . .' Then I remember talking to him on the phone several times when I was working in London, sometime right before 9/11. He continued the same theme. He said something like, 'Live your life right now, in the moment . . . you never know when your number's up.' He made a point of saying that again."

On September 2, 2001, Eamon and I and the children continued the family tradition of attending a barbecue and fireworks display that takes place on the day before Labor Day. Several members of Eamon's family came to visit and attend the event with us. As soon as his brother Patrick arrived, Eamon almost immediately began a conversation with him, discussing the possibility that there would be another terrorist attack on the World Trade Center. Eamon was convinced that the buildings would be struck again and soon. He knew that people would look to him for guidance in how to best get out of the building, just as they had during the 1993 bombing, when he had led more than sixty fellow employees in a darkened, smoke-filled stairwell down the hundred-plus flights from his office. Should he tell them to walk down the stairs or head straight up to the roof? Eamon and

Patrick actually debated the question of which escape route would be best this time while the rest of us listened, not knowing quite what to say. The discussion ultimately ended with the notion that the roof might be best—assuming there would be helicopters to rescue everyone.

Within the next day or so, Eamon expressed another concern.

"Bonnie," he said to me, "you'd better start applying more discipline to the children, because when I'm gone, you're going to have a hard time."

"But you're the disciplinarian," I answered.

"Yes," he replied, "but I'm not going to be here that long."

I didn't know how to respond when Eamon made this kind of statement. I remember initially laughing his comments off. I would say things like, "Oh, Eamon, please stop with this." I once remember saying, "You are such a pessimist."

"No," he responded. "You'll find out."

Tuesday evening, September 4th, Eamon came home from his long commute and disappeared into the den. When he emerged, I was standing at the kitchen stove, making pasta for dinner. He looked at me with a strange expression on his face—as if he was focusing on something in the far distance. "I'm going to die before you," he announced in a matter-of-fact manner.

"Come on, Eamon," I replied, once more treating his comments lightly. He moved closer to me, with his face just a few inches from mine. He had a habit of doing this when he wanted to make a point. He forced me to look deep into his eyes. They were such a beautiful, alluring blue.

"I'm going to die before you," he repeated. "I just want you to know that," and he turned and walked out of the room.

I remember thinking that his warning was particularly intense and odd, but I didn't know how to respond, so I shrugged it off. Nonetheless, I was beginning to be more concerned about Eamon's state of mind. I was worried. I wondered if he was sinking into some kind of clinical depression.

Several days passed, and then Friday morning, September 7th, arrived. As I did every morning, I woke up to the 5:00 A.M. alarm. Eamon got up grudgingly and jumped into the shower, muttering how much he hated going down to the "coal mine" every day. He got dressed in the early morning light as I lay on my side of the bed, listening to him move around the room. I could see dawn's rose-colored reflection in the mirror above the bureau; delicate pink fingers were wrapped gently around the clouds. It could just as easily have been dusk—the glow of different shades of fuchsia, white, and red blending together so softly, so peacefully.

Eamon headed to the door of our bedroom and stopped short. I looked up at him and saw that same distant look that I had noticed three days earlier.

"You know, every morning, when we leave for work," he said, "we don't know if we'll return." He paused for a minute. "We have to make the best of every day that we are given."

And with that, he left. The fact that Eamon had made so many similar comments within the last few days was disconcerting. I remember thinking, "What is up with him?"

The rest of Friday and Saturday passed in a blur, but then on Sunday night, September 9th, once again Eamon seemed preoccupied. I remember we were down in the children's playroom, watching the second episode of the World War II miniseries *Band of Brothers*. It was the premier airing. This particular episode focused on the June 6th, 1944, invasion of Normandy, better known as D-day. It featured a group of American paratroopers, Company E, parachuting out of their planes to join the effort to liberate Europe. Eamon, who had been watching intently, suddenly turned to me.

"They must have been so afraid," he spoke very calmly. "Many of them were only seventeen." Then he gently placed his hand on my arm and made another strange statement. "I want you to know," he told me, "that I think I can handle my death now."

I was taken aback by the sincerity of his statement. I could no longer dismiss his concerns or pretend that they were some kind of bizarre joke. I could feel the tears welling up in my eyes.

"Eamon, stop talking this way," I pleaded. "I love you so much, please . . ." All I could think about were the lines of fatigue that framed the corners of his eyes and his exhausting and grueling commute to work each day. When I looked at him, once again he seemed to be staring off into the distance.

"Don't go downtown anymore," I pleaded. It was a request I had made many times since the '93 World Trade Center bombing, but with far less emotion. "You don't have to work there. . . . I know you hate working in that building."

It took everything I had to keep from crying. Eamon turned away from me and focused back on the television. Following 9/11, I spent a lot of time thinking about all of Eamon's premonitions. I couldn't help but wonder why he was so certain that he was going to die. And why was he so spiritually strong? Who was guiding him, and how was he getting his information?

After Eamon's death, I also couldn't help thinking about the strong bond that existed among the paratroopers in *Band of Brothers* and, similarly, the close friendships my husband and his coworkers shared. At the end, it was perhaps a sense of duty, but it was also the love and respect they felt for their comrades that was so important to both groups of men in facing their unknown outcomes. Regardless of what Eamon had shared with me about being ready to face his death, I'm sure he was afraid. However, I'd like to think that being surrounded by that group of very special men, whom he had known and cared about for so many years, helped him more than I will ever know.

During the fall of 2001, I was developing closer relationships with other 9/11 families. We understood so much about each other's pain; it was natural that we would gather together for support and encouragement. I was curious whether anybody else had premonitions such as Eamon's. In the course of talking about this, people started telling me about spiritual experiences they associated with their losses, some more unusual than others. One friend heard music coming from an empty room; another believed that she saw her husband standing at the door; several had unusual experiences with birds and butterflies; a large number talked about finding objects in unfamiliar places. The fact that so many of us were experiencing similar phenomena made it all the more remarkable and more difficult to disregard or dismiss as coincidence.

One friend in particular, Kate*, shared that whenever she thought of her son or missed him most, she would find a penny, often in an unusual location; once, at a 9/11 legal meeting, while thinking about her son, she looked down, and there was one right by her foot. Finding these pennies gave her a sense that she and her son still shared a spiritual connection.

A few months after 9/11, I received a phone call at work from a man named John Duffy, who, along with his brother Michael, knew Eamon as fellow lacrosse players. I had met them both.

"I have some checks for you," John said, "and I have something to tell you."

John said that he and Michael, had been very upset to hear about Eamon's death, and that Michael felt that he had to do something—anything—to make life easier for me and my children. Michael, who was living in California, decided that he was going to run in three consecutive marathons—three full marathons in three days—and that, by doing so, he would try to raise money to help my family. John would make the fund-raising phone calls. As John started telling me this, I was both moved and amazed by Michael's spontaneous and generous spirit. How kind and caring! And how amazing that Michael, at the age of forty-four, would attempt this kind of athletic feat!

John told me that the races were extremely difficult for Michael and that after the second one, Michael was totally exhausted. When he got back to his room, he was so tired that he had to crawl to the bathroom. Then he looked up and saw Eamon standing there in the corner of the room, encouraging him to continue. Michael told John that Eamon spoke to him, telling him that it was important for him to finish that last race. Michael was as inspired as he was stunned, and he went on to run the third race and to get his best time in doing so.

"You mean Michael actually saw Eamon?" I asked.

"That's what he said," John replied.

I couldn't ask Michael about this myself because John had some other tragic news. Not long after these races, Michael was driving a car during a rainstorm. He was going rather slowly, but nonetheless the car skidded off the road and crashed into a tree. Michael's passenger walked away from the crash, but Michael, who was hit by a large tree branch, was killed.

I was shocked by what he told me. I knew how close John and Michael were, and I felt so badly for him and his family. I was also extraordinarily touched by Michael's big-hearted kindness and generosity in wanting to help my family. As for the story of Michael having seen Eamon, I didn't know what to say or believe, but I couldn't help reflecting on the lacrosse brotherhood. Eamon knew what a great athlete Michael was. He always loved coaching and supporting his friends. Despite Eamon's death, the connection with Michael remained.

Around Christmas 2001, my children and I went to Florida. While there, I ran into Ed and Maureen Lunder. Ed Lunder had been Eamon's boss a number of years before at a different Wall Street firm. Their son Chris, another Cantor employee, had died on 9/11. I was surprised to learn that Ed and Maureen had visited several mediums and were very impressed with what they heard. The Lunders are so credible that I couldn't help paying attention to what they had to say.

While in Florida, I also had another spiritual experience. It was early in the morning—just after dawn; I was walking on a road parallel to the beach, feeling very sad and burdened, when suddenly I got the sensation that Eamon was walking right beside me. But he wasn't alone. Walking around me were other loved ones who had died in earlier years. My father was there; another friend was there. It felt as though I was surrounded by people who I had been very close to at different times in my life. They were all telling me to be strong and that everything was going to be all right. It was an amazing and important moment in my life that I will never forget.

In February of 2002, just a few days before my birthday, I was at a small meeting in a neighboring town with several others who had lost loved ones on 9/11. A knock on the door interrupted us. It was my pastor and a police officer I knew; they were there to tell me that some of Eamon's remains had been located. I had come to accept the reality that Eamon's body would probably never be recovered. Hearing the news, I was thrown somewhat into a state of shock. When the pastor and I left the meeting together, he instinctively got into the driver's seat. We spoke very little as he drove. Vaguely I noticed a cemetery sign ahead of us. That's when I realized that the pastor had taken this route intentionally.

"Let's drive through," he said before reminding me, "You have to start thinking about this. You'll need to decide what to do with the remains. This is a lovely cemetery—very peaceful."

Driving in the car with my pastor, I felt as if I were living in a surreal world. It was very similar to how I felt in the days after the World Trade Center crumbled—that sense of going through the motions without really connecting to the experience. Entering the cemetery with the understanding that I might want to bury Eamon there didn't feel real. "Eamon is dead," I thought. "They have found his body." I had the sensation that we were floating. The day itself was rainy and gray with the kind of chill that goes right through your clothing. "They found Eamon," I repeated to myself. So many months had passed. How could that be? Losing Eamon still seemed totally unbelievable to me. He went to work one day and just disappeared—poof! Just like that! Never to be seen again. I assumed that was how my children were processing everything. Daddy went to work and never came back. He simply evaporated.

As the pastor and I slowly drove through the cemetery entrance, I saw something large in the air zoom right down in front of my car. The pastor had to brake quickly to keep from hitting it. I stared in disbelief. It was a great blue heron. The bird organized his wings for a few seconds and then just stood there—proudly holding up his head with that bluish gray crown of feathers. The color reminded me of the early morning fog that meandered through the vineyards of Northern California. He was majestic. "Oh my God," I thought. I knew that blue herons spanned a wide geographic area from Canada to Florida, but they prefer a warmer climate. To see one in our Connecticut town in the bitter, biting cold of February was not normal—especially in a cemetery.

The great blue heron was the one bird that had significance in my life. When my parents lived in Florida, a great blue heron patrolled the water's edge in front of their home. In the morning, as my father was having breakfast, he would always look out the window to check on the bird's whereabouts. Inevitably, it would show up, its majestic silhouette outlined against the morning sun. There was such a connection between my father and the heron that one Christmas Eamon and I bought him a stunning replica of a heron from Steuben Glass.

After my father died, whenever Eamon or I saw a blue heron, we were reminded of my father and the time we'd spent together. For me, the bird was particularly meaningful because it was a point of connection between Eamon and my father. When I saw it in the cemetery, I felt it was a spiritual sign that this was the correct place to lay Eamon to rest, and it gave me a measure of peace at a very nonpeaceful time.

The blue heron helped me choose a cemetery for Eamon, but I still needed to decide exactly where he should be buried. The only other time I saw the bird was several weeks later when I returned to the cemetery to select a burial plot. My friend Lori came with me;

she and her husband had known Eamon for over twenty years. I felt comfortable having her help me select the best possible grave site, but we were having trouble picking one out. The chief administrator of the cemetery was driving us, and he kept stopping at location after location. We would get out of the car and stand on the available site to see how we felt about it. Nothing felt right. How could it? I was having a difficult time believing what I was doing. It felt like a nightmare. How could I possibly be searching for the right place to bury my husband? Did all of this really happen?

Finally, our guide had another thought. "I've been taking you to all the newer locations that are available," he said. "Let me show you one of the older areas."

He drove us down the hill and to the right of where we had been looking. "There," he pointed, "what about that area? See, over there."

Lori and I got out of the car once more and walked up a slight incline to the place he was recommending. We stood there, breathing in the cold air. I shut my eyes and felt a new warmth flow through my body as the sun broke through the clouds. When I looked up, there it was. The great blue heron! Lori, whom I had already told about the earlier sighting, now saw it, too. It was right in front of me again, next to where the car was parked. The bird had come out of nowhere. It seemed impossible that we had neither heard nor seen him land, given the breadth of his wingspan.

"Lori, where did he come from?" I asked.

"I have no idea," she replied. She was just as amazed as I was.

We both knew that this was where Eamon would be buried. It was the perfect place. I felt a sense of peace. In all my many trips to visit Eamon's grave, I never again saw the great blue heron.

Other things were also happening in my own life that I couldn't understand—and that were giving me a sense that Eamon was somehow still looking out for his family. I can't explain, for example, how his wedding band was found and returned to me. It's a puzzle ring, with four thin interlocking gold bands. How could it have been found in the still-burning pile at Ground Zero? But it was. Eamon's cousin John Beggins, a New York City police officer assigned to guard Cardinal Egan, was the one who brought me the ring. When I opened the velvet box he handed me, I could see that the ring had come undone, but all the pieces had been found and were intact. Two of the bands were just slightly bent, and there was no hint of any of the gold melting. In a few seconds, I manipulated the pieces and had the ring back in its original form. To me, having this ring returned was a miracle. I viewed it as another "sign" and a message from my husband—a message that everything would be okay and that I could get on with my life.

Several years passed and I had no additional experiences like those I'd had in the time immediately following 9/11. I was beginning to question much of what I had previously believed to be spiritual events. Had my experiences and those of so many others all just been our imaginations at work—because we wanted so desperately to feel we still had a connection with the loved ones we lost? My growing skepticism was brought to a halt, however, in the summer of 2006.

It was a warm evening in July, and I was having dinner with several friends at a dining club. I had already started working on this book, but earlier that day, I had been having serious doubts about the project. It was a beautiful night, and we were seated outside on the patio. September 11th came up in conversation, as it so often does. Sitting next to me was a well-known local surgeon, and I started telling him about my friend Kate, and the pennies she continued to find. I then segued over to the premonitions that Eamon had shared before his death. The doctor had known Eamon and was interested, as were several others at the table who began paying attention to our conversation.

I had just finished telling the doctor about the comments Eamon had made while watching the D-day episode of *Band of Brothers* when the waiters appeared with menus. They were fairly heavy, so we each placed them down as soon as they were handed to us. Still deep in conversation, as I opened mine, I saw the doctor looking across at it. Out of the corner of my eye, I noticed that the man sitting on my left was also looking at it with a very surprised expression on his face. When I looked down, I couldn't believe what I saw. There was a penny sitting in the middle of my menu. A chill ran through my body. "Oh Eamon," I thought. "It's really true. You really are here." Did Eamon know I was reverting back to a skeptical mind-set? I wondered. Was this his attempt to prevent that from happening?

We all stared at the penny. "It looks old," said the doctor. I put on my reading glasses and tried to make out the date, but the coin was very worn. We could see the ONE CENT printed on the back bordered by the two sprigs of wheat, indicating that it was an older penny. Unfortunately it was too dark to make out the date.

Later, as we continued to talk, Rick, another man at the table, told me that after his father died, his mother started to find dimes, usually four at a time, grouped together. The circumstances under which she found them were so unusual that she was convinced that they represented messages from her husband.

When I got home later that evening, a friend from dinner was with me. We were both curious about the date on the penny; as soon as we walked through the door, I went to my desk to get a magnifying glass. At the moment I found the coin in the menu, I had been talking about Eamon's premonitions as we were watching the D-day episode of *Band of Brothers*. At home, I looked through the glass and gasped. The date on the penny was 1944, the year of D-day.

I racked my brain, trying to find logical reasons how this penny would appear in my menu. Because it was a dining club, there were absolutely no cash transactions. People were required to sign for everything. Could somebody have been discussing a coin collection and by accident left this particular coin on their menu, only to have it fall into the sleeve when the waiter picked it up? That seemed too far-fetched. Besides, most coin collectors have mint or newer-looking coins. Could someone have been playing a practical joke, inserting the penny in the menu that was meant for me? That also seemed ridiculous, because none of the people at the table had that kind of dark humor. How would any of them have been able to find a 1944 penny that quickly? There is no way anybody could have anticipated a conversation about Eamon's premonitions involving the date 1944. I was also positive that none of them had any earlier knowledge about Kate's penny experiences, so how would they know to play a joke like that? In this case, the more believable explanation was that the penny was Eamon's way of letting me know that he was still watching out for us and to not be skeptical.

A few months later, I was at a party that was attended by Rick's brother, Brad, who was one of the top people at the State Department under Condoleezza Rice. When Brad and I started talking, I shared my penny story and asked him about the coins that were found by his family after his father's death. Brad pulled out his wallet and took out an index card that had four dimes taped to it. "It's true," Brad told me. He went on to say that he had been sufficiently moved by the unusual circumstances in which these coins had been found, that he had put them into his wallet and kept them there as a good-luck token and reminder of his father. They had traveled with him on all his State Department trips, including those he made to the war zones of Iraq and Afghanistan.

This past year, Eamon's family had some bad news. His older sister Laurie, living in Nevada, was diagnosed with cancer. A couple of months after this diagnosis, she called to share a special story with me. Apparently someone she knew had had an experience concerning Eamon and after-death communication. In this case, it was Laurie's best friend's daughter, Cathleen Barnett. A few weeks later I called Cathleen to hear more of the details.

Cathleen knew Eamon because they had both worked at the same company for over a year. It was one of her first jobs after school, and she says that she remembered him always being very kind to her. Without hesitation Cathleen told me her story. "It was in December, and it was after eleven o'clock at night," she said. "I was lying in bed, saying my rosary. I do this every night. I had just gotten to the part where I pray for everyone I know who has passed away. I've been doing this for as long as I can remember. I started praying for Eamon right after he died. I used to list everyone individually, but as I've gotten older and the list has gotten longer, most of the time, I just pray for them all together.

"Anyway, just then, I heard a man's voice saying, 'Laurie!' It was very loud. I looked up, and there, standing right between my window and closet door, I saw Eamon. He was wearing a suit, and he looked just like he did when we worked together. He was there for less than a minute, and then he faded away.

"My first thought was, did my husband, who was asleep next to me, hear him? But he didn't even wake up. The next morning I called my mother and asked her if she had spoken to Laurie. I said, 'Could you call her please?' My mother wanted to know why. I told her, 'I know you're not going to believe me, but this is what happened.' I was concerned that Eamon wanted me to tell Laurie something. I wanted to make sure that Laurie was okay." When Cathleen's mother called Laurie to tell her what had happened, Laurie said that she was fine, but she was feeling a little tired.

Within the next couple of weeks, Laurie went to the doctor and received her surprise cancer diagnosis.

Cathleen said that she had never before had an experience like the one she did when she saw Eamon, but that she wasn't at all frightened. She said that she felt honored that he had chosen her to deliver a message. She felt that Eamon wanted Laurie to know that he was looking out for her and that she shouldn't be frightened.

I find it startling that people have seen Eamon since his death. I also find it interesting to think about the circumstances under which these events take place, whether they are happening to strangers or touch me personally. It defies human logic. We don't understand any of this, and yet there is no question in my mind that something extraordinary is taking place.

It also sometimes seems as though Eamon is actually helping me make decisions and advising me. Not that long ago, I received word that Roy Simmons Jr., the retired star coach of the Syracuse lacrosse team, had lost his wonderful wife. Roy taught Eamon much about life, great writers, and also folk art. I know Eamon cherished their friendship. Ever since 9/11, Roy had faithfully sent us maple syrup and cheddar cheese from upstate New York at Christmastime. I had never met Roy's wife, but he sent me the program from her funeral, which helped me understand a bit more about what a special woman she was.

When I started composing a condolence note to Roy in my head, I was at a loss for words. Finally, I went into the closet to find an appropriate note card, and a bunch of papers fell off the shelf. I picked them up and noticed that one of them was a poem my husband had written for Roy that I had never seen before. It was entitled "Streams of Friends—For Roy Simmons." Of course I was shocked. Then I understood and did what I knew Eamon wanted me to do: I sent Roy the poem, again reminding him of their unbroken friendship. The last lines of the poem are:

> *Conversations meet no rocks*
> *& rapids are never whirlpools*
> *In streams of friends*

I was reminded of something someone said to me while working on this book: "Just because someone's life has ended doesn't mean the relationship has to end."

Eamon and Bonnie

The family *(left to right)*:
(back) Eamon, Kyle, Brendan, Kevin, and Bonnie;
(front) Jennifer

PART TWO

THE UNBROKEN CONNECTION

After my husband's death, I received an enormous amount of support from others who were also going through the grieving process. In the early days, there were 9/11 family members who talked regularly, sometimes even daily. Some of us noticed that strange events were taking place around us, and we tentatively began to share the details. Since the majority of those killed were men, at first I was mostly talking to other widows, mothers, daughters, and sisters. Later, I met some of the husbands, fathers, brothers, and sons. Although these men and women were all having different kinds of spiritual experiences, there is a dominant theme: They all feel that the messages they have received are those of assurance, comfort, and support.

These are some of the men and women who helped open my eyes to the possibility of a larger, more spiritual reality.

CHAPTER TWO

I'm Here . . . I'm Okay . . . I Love You

Joanne Kelly, Wife of James Kelly

*When the Cantor Fitzger-
ald wives I know talk to one
another, we always think
about the close friendships,
loyalty, and humor that
existed among our husbands,
some of whom had worked
together for many years. We
also remember the off-the-
wall jokes that "the boys"
couldn't resist "pulling." My
husband and his friends
would do just about anything
to get a single good laugh.
One of Eamon's best friends*

Joanne and Kells dancing

*at work was James Kelly, who everybody called Kells. He was thirty-nine
when he died, and he was an all-around great guy. Kells worked at three
different companies with Eamon, and they always tried to change jobs
together. Eamon and Kells had a favorite story about a day when Kells
stayed home from work. He got a phone call that night from Eamon. "Hi,*

Kells," Eamon said. "I guess you should know that I quit the job today, and, oh yeah, I quit for you, too."

"What!?" Kells replied.

"Don't worry," Eamon told him. "We both have new jobs. We're going to Cantor Fitzgerald."

K ells and his wife, Joanne, met in high school and had been together ever since. They have four daughters, two of whom are twins. Kells called all the girls "my squad." The twins had another special name. Kells referred to them as "the twinkies."

Joanne Kelly was one of the first people to tell me that she had a sense that her husband was trying to send her "messages" or "signs" to tell her that he was okay. These signs started appearing within days of 9/11. Hearing about them from somebody as down-to-earth as Joanne was very convincing. She is one of my favorite people. She's an incredibly warm, funny, honest, and good-hearted woman who takes care of everybody who crosses her path. When I told Jo that I was working on a book about paranormal experiences surrounding 9/11, she said that she would be happy to be interviewed. Jo had already told me that she was regularly finding coins that she identified as signs from her husband. In her case, dimes suddenly appear where none had been before. Almost as soon as we sat down to talk at the kitchen table at her house on Long Island, a dime flew out of nowhere, and landed on the floor between us. I have no idea where it came from. It literally just appeared.

The most amazing thing about Jo's story is that she has actually seen her husband's spirit when she has been wide awake and fully alert. When she discusses this, she is so matter-of-fact and straightforward that it makes her experience appear almost commonplace. I should also add that, even though we are friends, Jo didn't tell me the details about seeing Kells until I expressly asked her to tell me about *all* her experiences.

"The first time I saw Kells, he had been dead about six months," she said. "It was about ten-thirty or eleven o'clock at night. I was downstairs, and the thing that caught my attention was some movement I couldn't explain. Out of the corner of my eye I saw something in the hall. It moved so fast that it almost seemed to go *whoosh*. At first I got scared. I thought maybe somebody got into the house, so I went from room to room to make sure nobody was there. I went upstairs and checked on all the girls. They were sleeping. I decided it was my imagination and came back down to watch the news and wait for Leno to come on. During a commercial break, I decided to get up and get something in the kitchen. That's when I saw Kells. I saw his back first. Then he turned around. When he looked at me, he had a smile on his face. I was so surprised that I don't think I said anything. He was just there for a few seconds. Then he walked toward the door and disappeared."

When I asked her what Kells was wearing, Jo described him in detail. "He was dressed like he always was. He was wearing his baseball cap turned backward, a T-shirt and shorts. He looked exactly the same as he did the night before 9/11. I always remember that night. He was going out for a jog. One of the girls needed something for school, which meant one of us had to go to the store. When this kind of thing came up, we usually flipped a coin, but Kells tried to talk me into going. He said, 'I'll buy. You fly.' That meant that I would be the one who would go to the store. I remember saying, 'No way. You flip that coin.' When I saw Kells in my kitchen in 2002, he looked almost exactly as he had on September 10th. He looked good."

I asked Jo if she felt frightened or nervous when she saw her husband's spirit. "No," she answered. "I always felt safe with Kells. And I always trusted him. Completely! I knew he could be counted on to take care of us. There was a safeness about my marriage, and this was no different. It was Kells. I was glad to see him. He was there, and we were safe." Jo wasn't afraid of her husband's spirit, but she was a little bit nervous about what people would think if she told them about some of the things that have happened in her house. She didn't want others questioning either her sanity or the validity of what she knew she experienced. She shared the details with her mother, whom she trusted, but not many others. "I can always feel Kells, and I know that he is here with us. Sometimes I even smell his cologne," Jo assured me.

Jo was on the phone, talking to her husband, when American Airlines Flight 11 hit the North Tower. She heard a loud sound coming from his end. "Jo!" Kells said. "Turn on the TV! I think something hit us. We've got a lot of smoke up here." She could hear the excited voices of the guys he worked with in the background.

"What's going on?" she asked him. She thought she heard the phone drop. And then the line went dead. She tried frantically to call him back, but there was no answer. Jo says that she was so upset she fell on her knees. "I had such a pain in my chest that I thought I was having a heart attack," she told me. "I knew immediately that he was gone."

Within twenty-four hours of Kells's death, two white doves arrived in her yard and sat near the pool. As Jo looked at these two doves, all she could think about was Kells and how much she missed him. She was trying to keep things together for the sake of her children, but she was inconsolable. The doves were the first of many signs.

Jo wasn't sure what to make of the doves, but soon thereafter she talked to one of her neighbors, an older man. He told her how sorry he was about her husband's death, but he also told her that she should now expect to see white doves around her house, and that this is a common "sign" when someone dies. On Thanksgiving 2001, Jo took her children first to her parents' house for dinner. Then they went to her in-laws for dessert. It was an extremely sad day, with everyone missing Kells. When it was time for Jo and the children to go home, they walked out to the car. There, on the roof of the car, was a white dove. Someone went to get a camera and take a picture. Jo wouldn't leave until the dove flew off on its own.

Some of the most common signs Jo receives come in the form of blinking lights. She had so many problems with her lights after Kells's death that she kept calling the electrician, who told her, "There is nothing wrong with your electricity." Blinking lights are still a common occurrence. Within the last few months, for example, Jo was sitting at her kitchen table with a friend. Jo's daughters were also in the room. Suddenly, a kitchen light on the wall flickered. Then a light in the hallway did the same, followed by yet another light on the ceiling. Jo checked the bulbs and the fuses; nothing was wrong, and there was no explanation.

"Maybe it's Daddy," her ten-year-old daughter said. "Daddy, if it's you," she continued, "blink three times." Within seconds the light above the kitchen table flickered three times. Jo and her children are accustomed to this kind of event, but Jo's friend was a little bit spooked. "I'm getting out of here!" she said.

Jo's experience with flickering lights isn't limited to what goes on inside her home. On the street outside her house, for example, is a city streetlight. In the evening, Jo walks her dog around the block. Frequently when she does so, the light goes out as soon as she leaves the driveway. It doesn't come back on again until she returns. Jo likes to think that her husband is taking a walk with her.

In the first month after the attack on the World Trade Center, as one would expect, Jo was grief stricken. She wanted to know exactly what had happened to her husband and how he'd died; she also felt he was trying to tell her something or leave her some sign of his presence. She was particularly upset by a recurring dream in which her husband had taken off his shirt and was attempting to tie it and other shirts together, trying to find a way out of the burning building. On September 29th, she went to visit a psychic named Jeffrey Wands, who was located on Long Island.

"When I made the appointment," she said, "I made a point of not telling him anything about who I was or why I was calling, but the minute I got there, I felt as though Jeffrey Wands 'got' me. He told me that I had lost my soul mate and my heart and soul were broken beyond repair at that time. He told me that my husband never had a broken bone in his body (which was true). He also said that Kells was a clean pure soul—a 'golden' soul—who was immediately accepted into heaven. But Wands said that Kells didn't want to go because he didn't want to leave his *squad*."

Jo was really impressed by the use of the word *squad*, because that's exactly what Kells called their daughters. "Wands asked me if Kells was a fireman, because he saw him running around trying to find a way out with other people following his lead. I told him that Kells was one of the floor fire marshals, and that he took these duties very seriously. Do you remember?" Jo asked me, "how he always complained that there was no sprinkler system on the floor?"

"Wands said that Kells was with his *brothers* when he died, and that's exactly how Kells thought of the guys he worked with," Jo continued. "Wands also said that Kells didn't suffer, and that he wasn't wearing a shirt. It took me a long time to put together my dream of him without a shirt to what Wands said."

There were other things that Jeffrey Wands said that connected to Jo's experience. "He told me that there would be a lot of butterflies. That year, there were butterflies in my backyard as well as all those butterflies that showed up at the Ground Zero site. And Wands talked to me about seeing blinking lights and how that was Kells way of letting us know that he was around. He said that spirits were often able to 'rearrange electricity.' Wands also said that it was going to be exceptionally warm that year because God was looking out for his souls."

For a while, Jo admits that she found herself psychic hopping. More than anything else, she wanted to maintain her connection to her beloved husband. On one occasion, she was able to get tickets to a John Edward taping; he quickly identified her as a 9/11 widow.

"Edward said he saw me in a house with a lot of green," Jo recounted, "and anyone who has ever been in my house knows that it is filled with green colors. Edward was also the first person to talk about all the dimes I was finding. He said, 'You must be rich because he is leaving you dimes everywhere.'"

Jo was particularly impressed by something else John Edward told her about her children. He said that Kells wanted to acknowledge her twins, calling them, as Kells did, "the twinkies."

After doing a reading on camera, John Edward asked Jo to meet with him in the green room after the taping. There he told her that he realized she was visiting a lot of psychics, and that he would advise her to stop because he didn't think it was good for her or good for her husband's spirit, saying that Kells was using up a lot of his energy. She took this advice very much to heart.

Jo tries to stay positive and upbeat. Initially she was worried about the prospect of raising her children without their father, but she feels that Kells usually finds a way to let her know that he is with her, particularly at those times that she feels most discouraged and alone. She and the children, for example, took a trip to Hershey, Pennsylvania. This was something they had done in the past with Kells. At one point when they were there, her oldest daughter wanted to go on a roller-coaster ride. Her daughter and Jo were both sad. "The last time I went on this ride, Daddy was with me," her daughter said. Jo, who had walked with her to stand on line, looked down at the ground. There, at her feet, was a shining dime.

"Don't worry," Jo assured her daughter. "You'll be safe. Daddy is still here."

By 2004, the Kelly family had still not received any remains for burial, which was distressing for everyone. Kells's parents, as well as his brother and sister, made an appointment with the medical examiner to take a tour of the facility and get a better understanding of how remains were being identified. At first Jo wasn't going to accompany them, but at the last minute she changed her mind. Since 2001, there had been some new advances in DNA testing. For that reason, Jo had already swabbed her daughters' mouths in case samples of their DNA might help the process.

When they arrived at the place where workers were diligently trying to match victims' DNA, they were taken to a conference room. The medical examiner greeted them and began to explain the process and how things were being done.

Suddenly, Jo noticed that the lights over her head were blinking. Something was definitely going on with the lights. "Do you see the lights?" she asked. There was no response. Jo asked again, "Doesn't anybody see what's happening with the lights?" As she first started to speak, Jo felt forceful and strong, but then she began to be overcome with a new sensation. She became light-headed and felt as though she were going to faint. She was sure her husband was present with them. "He's here!" she exclaimed. "Look at the lights! He's here!" Her mother-in-law, recognizing her agitation, tried to calm her down. "Don't worry, honey," she said. "Maybe we'll get some answers."

At that exact moment, there was a knock on the door. The medical examiner left the room. When he returned, he had a shocked expression on his face. They had just, at that very moment, made a positive identification of Kells's remains. The medical examiner told them that this was a first: they had never before made such an identification while the victim's family was present.

Jo walked outside with the group to the area where the refrigerated trucks that held the remains were kept. There were about six eighteen-wheel trucks parked there. That's when Jo got another strange feeling. "He's in that truck," she said, pointing to one of them. She could sense where her husband's remains were located. She was correct. She and the family wanted to do something to acknowledge the spiritual significance of this moment. Her mother-in-law had a Mass prayer card in her pocket from the service they had held for Kells. The workers, who Jo said were incredibly kind, let them tape it on the truck. Somebody from the medical examiner's office gave them a votive candle, which they lit outside the closed door of the truck that held Kells's remains; they all said a prayer.

Jo tells a story about her husband that reflects the kind of person he was. Soon after they'd first moved into their house, Kells noticed the elderly woman who lived next door struggling to carry her groceries into her house. Kells immediately ran over to help her. "Just remember," he said to his new neighbor, "you've got a pair of strong arms next door to help. Call us if you need anything." Jo continued her friendship with this neighbor after Kells died. In fact, Jo helped care for her when she was sick. During her neighbor's final illness, Jo made a request of the woman, who talked often of dying. "When you get there," Jo said, "I know you are going to see Kells. Try to give me a sign—so I know you are there." Twenty-four hours after the woman passed over, Jo was looking out the window. That's when she saw the white dove fly out of the sky and land on her neighbor's roof.

Jo didn't really expect to see Kells's spirit again, but this past Christmas Eve, once more, he was there. It was very similar to the first time: He was wearing his baseball cap backward and standing in their kitchen. Jo was very happy to see him.

"In my heart I know Kells is always with us," she said. "There are always things that remind me of his presence. They may just seem coincidental, but there are too many of them. A few weeks ago, it was my daughter's birthday, and I went to the cemetery. It was a bitter cold day, so I didn't stay long. I got in the car, and I was feeling sad that my daughter is growing up without her father. On the way home, in my car, all of sudden all this white mist starts coming out of my vents. I couldn't figure out what it could be. It was too cold for my car to be heating up. The funny thing about this though is that it didn't smell like smoke or anything. It was white and there was no odor. I was nervous about driving, so I pulled over and turned the car off, and I started talking to Kells. 'Is it you?' I asked him. I start the car and the mist fades away. 'If it is you, Kells,' I say, 'just give me a sign. Give me something.' I start the car and there is no more smoke, but then as I'm driving home, I switch radio stations, and our wedding song, 'You're Just too Good to Be True,' by Frankie Valli and the Four Seasons comes on. I said out loud, 'Kells, it was you!' And I honestly think it was. By the way, this kind of thing never happened with the car before or since. I knew it was him, and it made so me so happy I started to sing along.

"I have a picture of Kells near my bed. Every day when I wake up I say, 'Good morning, honey.' Kells was my best friend. I always loved him with my whole heart, and I always will. We were together for so long that we could finish each other's sentences. He was my right hand; he was my left hand. He was everything to me. I just knew he would always be there for me and our family. The thing about Kells though is that he was always there for anybody who needed him."

The last Kelly family photograph
(left to right): (back) Jo and Kells;
(middle) Brianne, Katie, and Erin;
(front) Colleen

Deborah Calandrillo, Wife of Joseph Calandrillo

Joseph Calandrillo

People who knew Deborah and Joseph Calandrillo always comment on the same three things: how much in love Deborah and Joe were with each other; how kind and thoughtful Joe was to those around him; and how devoted Deborah has been in keeping her husband's memory alive. On the night the couple first met, Joe hurried home to tell his family that he had met the woman he planned to marry. Joe was a tall, handsome man who had played minor league baseball, served in the army, and remained in top athletic shape throughout his life. He worked in the North Tower as an accountant at Reinsurance Solutions International, part of Marsh & McLennan.

When I first spoke with Deborah on the phone to make an appointment to talk, she told me that immediately prior to 9/11, her husband had been very focused on death. Joe, who was forty-nine, told her that he did not believe that he would make it to his fiftieth birthday. He said this often. When we sat down across from each other, Deborah, a very charming and graceful woman, elaborated about some specifics concerning fears and premonitions that they'd both experienced.

"One night, the first week of September, after I had gone to sleep, Joe woke me up," Deborah told me. "He was standing at the foot of our bed. He looked at me very intently and said, 'Deborah, I have a feeling that I'm going to die young.' That same week, he woke up again after having a terrible nightmare. He was almost trembling. He just hugged me and said, 'Debbie-Doodle'—that's what he called me—'don't let anything happen to you.'"

Deborah assured me that Joe never discussed his dreams, let alone a nightmare. "I told him that nothing was going to happen to me, but when I tried to find out what his dream was about, he wouldn't tell me. He said that it was 'too horrible to relate.'"

Given the level of closeness in Deborah and Joe's marriage, it's not strange that she also experienced an unusual dream in the week preceding 9/11. In her dream, Deborah woke up to a noise from somewhere in her house. She walked down the hallway toward the sound that she heard. She proceeded into a room and pulled up the shade of a very small window. "I realized it was an airplane window," she said. "And when I looked out, I saw the extension of our house. It was much closer than in reality, and I could see the top of the roof. There were two men crouched on the roof. They had dark brown hair, big brown eyes, and lightly tanned skin. Then I woke up."

Deborah said that after 9/11 she had frequent dreams about her husband, and that Joe always appeared despondent. In one dream Deborah remembers, she and her husband were sitting next to each other in an auditorium crowded with hundreds of people. Joe's eyes were full of tears. "I put my hand over his heart and told him, 'You were dead, but you are not dead anymore. In my dream, I thought my love for him was so powerful that it could pull him back from the dead.'"

Then, on March 10, 2002, on the eve of the six-month anniversary of 9/11, Deborah had another dream about Joe, but this one was different. "This time he was smiling," she said. "I was relieved when I woke up, thinking maybe now he is resting in peace."

The very next day, on March 11th, the City of New York hosted a service of remembrance, which she attended. When the service ended, she walked by herself to a special viewing area that had been set up for family members so they could look directly down on the site. As she was staring down, she noticed that the workers had stopped what they were doing and were lining up on both sides of the ramp that connected the base of Ground Zero with the street above. She didn't understand what was going on until she saw several stretchers, draped with American flags. The workers had just discovered the remains of some 9/11 victims. Deborah watched the rescue workers, lining up along the two sides of the ramp and standing with bowed heads as the stretchers were ceremoniously carried up. Deborah bowed her head and began to pray. That night she learned that some of Joe's remains had been found and identified.

"Years later," Deborah told me, "another 9/11 widow called me and said, 'I had a dream about you and your husband.' I asked her, 'When?' and she told me, 'Last night.' That was our wedding anniversary." Deborah sighed. "The woman said that in her dream my husband told her to tell me that he is always with me."

I asked Deborah if she felt her husband's presence. "Yes," she replied. "I feel a comfort, something that is with me—something good.

"You know, one day I lost my car keys. I was packing up Joe's things to give to a charity. Soon after, I realized my keys were lost. After I looked and looked, I asked Joe to help me. Suddenly, I heard a jingle. I had dropped them in the box of his clothes—and when I pulled them out, the whole room lit up. It was like all the clouds were pulled back and the sun came bursting through. I could feel the sun on my face by the window."

Not all messages from departed loved ones have come through dreams. I've spoken to quite a few men and women who feel that they have actually seen their loved ones. Deborah, like Jo Kelly and so many others in this book, falls into this group. She has only had one such vision of her beloved husband, Joe. It was sometime between 3:00 or 4:00 A.M., about a week after 9/11. He appeared suddenly in the bedroom they had shared. She was lying in bed. He was sitting on the bed next to her with tear-filled eyes. His arm was draped around her pillow. There was a solemn expression on his face. Deborah told me that she is positive she was awake when this happened.

Deborah knows why her husband appeared this way. "He came to say good-bye. When I saw him, he wasn't solid. I could see through him. I could see the table and the lamp behind him. I could see the pillow behind him, and then he disappeared. He wanted me to know that there is another existence after this one." Deborah knows how much her husband loved her—how inseparable they were. She has no problem believing that if there was any way it could be done, Joe would do it; he would cross back over the divide, for even an instant, to reassure her that he was okay.

Deborah is an intelligent, competent, and resourceful woman who isn't given to fantasy. She is hard-working and realistic. She is a responsible person who goes to work every day at a demanding job. Concern about what people might think makes it difficult for many of those who lost loved ones to share some of their extraordinary and not easily explained experiences. When Deborah told me about seeing her husband after his death, her voice became so soft she could barely be heard. We both knew why she was whispering. She was understandably wary about talking about what had happened because she realized how others might react. A skeptic might question the experiences of her or any of the other people in this book. Yes, it is true that when Deborah saw her beloved husband, she was stricken with a deep and profound grief over the sudden and brutal loss of the

Deborah and
Joe Calandrillo

person with whom she shared everything. But she was no less grief stricken the night before his spirit came and sat on her bed or, for that matter, the night after. She missed him no less the day before, or probably any day since. Nonetheless, she isn't having visions of him on a daily or nightly basis. This was a special occurrence. That's what makes it such a remarkable event.

Monica Iken, Wife of Michael Patrick Iken

Monica Iken has been a leading voice for the relatives of those whose lives were lost on 9/11. After her husband, Michael Patrick Iken, who

worked for Euro-Brokers, died in the South Tower of the World Trade Center, she focused her energy on finding ways to honor the memory of her husband and the other victims. She is the founder and creator of September's Mission, which she envisioned as a way of memorializing victims through the development of a memorial park on the former World Trade Center site.

Monica and Michael Iken

Monica met Michael Iken after he spotted her sitting down at the end of a restaurant bar one Saturday evening. He tried to get her attention to buy her a drink, but Monica, who was there with a friend, Jennifer, couldn't see that far, and they never even made eye contact. Nonetheless, Michael was so taken with her that he told a friend that this was the woman he planned to marry. He returned to the same restaurant the following Saturday, September 11, 1999, and just waited, convinced she would return. Four hours later, Monica and Jennifer, who had been on their way someplace else, had to change their plans and dropped into the restaurant to get something to eat. This time Michael made sure they met; Michael and Monica ended up sitting there, talking, until three in the morning. "He was just glowing," she said, "and I knew he was the one." In October of 2000, a year later, they were married on a beach in St. Martin. Just as they were repeating their vows, a jet zoomed overhead so loudly that they had to wait until it passed. Michael looked at Monica and said, "We're jinxed." At the time, Monica said, "No, we're not!"

"I know that I was put on this earth for a reason, and part of my destiny was to marry Michael," Monica told me. "Several years before I met Michael, I was in an auto accident and had a serious head injury. I was knocked unconscious, and I saw my whole life flash before me in a matter of seconds. It was like watching a tape on fast-forward. That accident was life changing. Almost from the moment I regained consciousness, I had a gut feeling that I wasn't where I was supposed to be and I wasn't doing what I was supposed to be doing. Nothing was right, so I changed everything in my life. Among other things I changed careers and divorced my first husband. From that moment, every turn I made led me to Michael."

In some ways Michael and Monica were ideally suited, but in others they appeared to be very different. Monica has a firm belief in God; Michael, on the other hand, was a self-described atheist. It really worried Monica. "I remember the first time he told me that, I freaked. I felt as though it was my duty to teach him about God and heaven. Michael's disbelief had a strong effect on me. It kind of turned me into Miss Spirituality. Michael also told me and others that he always expected to die young. He was in a fight with God. I tried to get him to understand that God is there to help." Monica laughed.

"I would talk about heaven as though I really knew what I was talking about. I remember once telling him that heaven was a beautiful, peaceful place. Michael looked at me and said, 'And how do you know that?' I always felt a need to help him feel better about death and God—to reassure him that if anything happened to him, he would be OK. We talked about death and God all the time. I expected Michael to live a long time, but whenever he died, I didn't want it to happen without his having any beliefs."

One day, when Monica and Michael were in their apartment, a talk show came on the television. One of the guests was a medium, who was talking about the afterlife. The medium described it as being like a giant lunchroom cafeteria, where you could hang out with just about anybody you wanted. Monica told Michael about the show and said, "If anything ever happens to us, you'd better meet me in the lunchroom." Michael thought it was funny, but he agreed. Every now and then, the thought would cross Monica's mind again, and she would ask him, "Where are you going to meet me?" He always had the same answer: "In the lunchroom, Monica, in the lunchroom."

Monica told me that Michael began acting a little strangely during the summer of 2001. "Michael had a close friend who had already sent out invitations for a December wedding. Michael kept saying that he just couldn't see himself being there. When I heard him say that, I said, 'I don't know what you're talking about.' He said, 'I just don't see myself there.' He was kind of projecting that he wouldn't be around for some reason. He couldn't seem to get himself past September."

There were several instances of Michael's unusual behavior in the month or so before the WTC attacks. On Saturday, September 1st, Michael decided that they should drive up to Boston for the Labor Day weekend. Once there, they checked into a hotel near Logan airport.

"Michael was very strange," Monica remembered. "For one thing, I was taking all these pictures, and Michael refused to be in any of them. When I look at the roll of film from that weekend, it's like he's not there. For another, he was upset and wasn't acting normally about anything. We weren't connecting; I couldn't reach him; and I didn't know what was bothering him. He kept pacing back and forth. From the airport window, you could see the planes at Logan, and I kept taking pictures of them, but Michael just kept getting more and more upset for no reason. Finally he said, 'I've got to get out of here; we have to leave right now,' so we left on Sunday morning. We were supposed to stay the weekend." Monica reminded me that the hijackers were also in Boston that weekend. "He just wasn't himself," Monica recalled, "as if he knew something terrible was about to happen to him."

On Monday, September 10th, Monica told Michael that she was planning to be in New York City the following day to visit a sick family member. Once again, Michael became very upset. "No," he told her. "Don't come to New York. I don't want you in the city. I don't want to be worrying about you all day." Monica couldn't understand Michael's extreme distress. He seemed very down and depressed. Monica remembers telling him, "You're going to be fine; we're going to be fine. We're young. There is nothing wrong. We have our whole lives ahead of us." At the time, Monica couldn't understand her husband's strange mood. She now believes that on some level he was preparing himself.

The following morning, Michael called Monica to tell her that an airplane had gone into the North Tower, but that the South Tower was okay and he was fine. He asked her to call his family, and that's what she was doing when the plane hit the South Tower. "The TV was on, and I could see it out of the corner of my eye." Monica tried calling him back, but all she could get was a busy signal.

That night Monica fell into a disturbed sleep on the couch near the door, hoping against hope that her husband was still alive. In the early morning hours, she woke to see Michael standing at the door. She jumped up and ran to him and threw her arms around him. "I'm okay; everything is fine," he said. Monica could see the light around him. "I knew he was gone," she said. "I felt the finality of what he was saying." In a few brief seconds, he somehow managed to convey that he was gone, but that he was okay. She is still unsure about whether this was a dream or some kind of spiritual visitation. It felt very real, but she couldn't be sure.

After this happened, on the deepest level she was convinced that her husband was dead. Nonetheless, she hoped that it was just a dream, so as soon as the sun came up, she headed downtown to put him on the missing persons' list. "Even if you know in your heart that someone's not here, you don't give up hope," Monica explained. "One piece of me was saying he's gone. It's over. Another was saying, maybe it was just a dream. You can't give up. Just make sure."

Almost immediately things began happening around Monica that she interpreted as signs or messages. In the first weeks after her husband's death, for example, she was having a difficult time being home alone. Henry, a close friend of Michael's, invited her to stay with him and his family, which she sometimes did. Henry and his wife had a four-year-old son. One morning, the child told her that he saw Michael in his dream. This occurred more than once. "This little boy was so young that he couldn't really pronounce all his words," Monica said, "and he was still speaking with a lisp, but he told me things like, 'Michael took me for ice cream. He says to tell you that he's fine and he's with the angels.'" Monica got a tape recorder and taped what the little boy said. To Monica, the little boy's words rang true.

Monica believes other children have been conscious of Michael's presence. When starting September's Mission, she would sometimes visit one of its first supporters in DC. This woman had twins who were less than two years old and not yet speaking. When they saw Monica, both of the twins would often look past her and point, as though somebody were standing behind her or next to her. Monica believes that even if they didn't see a physical presence, they may have been aware of the light.

Monica had one other dream about Michael in those early months that she associates more closely with a visitation than a dream. "I was looking into a mirror, and I saw Michael's face," she told me. "It was very distinct and very clear." Another time, Monica felt Michael next to her in the bed. "I was wide awake. I wasn't dreaming." Monica has no problem believing that if we are open to it, there is some form of communication that exists between our earthly world and the world that lies beyond—on the other side.

In the course of several years, Monica saw a few psychic mediums who gave her what she thinks of as accurate information. Some of the most compelling messages Monica received concerned her step-father, Tom.

"A few weeks before September 11th, I decided that I really wanted Michael to see the videotape of my first wedding," Monica recounted. "It wasn't that I wanted him to see me marrying somebody else—I wanted him to see Tom, my stepfather, who walked me down the aisle at St. Patrick's Cathedral. For reasons I didn't understand at the time, I told Michael, 'I think you need to see him.' I had trouble convincing Michael. Finally my friend Jennifer helped me talk him into it. I remember saying to Michael, 'I really want you to see Tom's face. Take a good look at him.' I loved my stepfather very much. I thought of him as my earth angel. I always felt that God sent him to protect me. He died shortly after that first wedding, so he never met Michael. What I found interesting was before doing my eulogy at Michael's memorial, which was also at St. Patrick's, I was directed to sit in the very same seat that Tom sat in after he gave me away.

"After Michael died, I was really worried about him because he didn't believe in anything, I prayed to Tom to "please help him pass over, please help him get through."

At least two of the psychic mediums she saw—Glenn Dove and John Edward—picked up details concerning Michael and Tom. John Edward got Tom's name correctly and Glenn Dove accurately described his physical appearance, as well as his relationship to Monica, saying, "He's like your father, but he's not your father." Several psychics told Monica that Tom was there to guide Michael when he passed over.

Glenn Dove, who Monica saw more than a year after 9/11, also "knew" other details about Monica's life. What Monica remembers best is that Dove knew about her teenage nephew who had just died. Dove knew his name, and he was able to describe the nature of his illness and details about his death. He knew that Monica had asked Michael to help her nephew on the other side. He also knew that Monica was about to move.

Monica finds herself talking to Michael all the time, and she feels that he tries to answer her. Things happen that she interprets as signs. Also right after she moved out of the apartment they shared, she saw her husband's spirit once again. This time, there is no question in her mind that she was wide awake and that it really happened. It was shortly after she had put her husband's belongings away in a large chest. When she looked up, Michael was standing right there in her new home. "I knew it was him 'cause I saw the light," she said. "I saw him smiling at the foot of the bed. I think he wanted me to know that he was still there. I think he was acknowledging the move and that I was with him . . . I know I was awake because I remember saying 'thank you' to him." He had somehow conveyed to her that he was there and knew she was trying to live her life.

Monica has remarried, and she and her husband now have two children. Monica believes Michael helped her find a new partner. "I always talk to Michael and ask his advice," Monica said. "If I go to bed with something on my mind and ask for Michael's help, more often than not, I wake up with an idea of what I should do. When I met Bob, my new husband, I wanted to know if he would be right for me." Monica liked Bob a great deal, and they had many things in common. They also share a connection to 9/11. Bob is a firefighter, and his entire rescue squad was killed that day. The only reason he is still alive is that he had the day off. He responded to the emergency call to go to the WTC, but he arrived after the buildings fell.

One night as Monica was going to bed, she asked Michael a question: "How do I know if Bob's right for me? How do I know if he is the one?" Monica told me, "I know how nuts this sounds." Nonetheless, the following morning when she woke up, she is sure she received this message: "Ask to see his baby pictures."

Monica has had too many spiritual experiences to question this kind of advice, so the very first time she went with Bob to his parents, she asked his mother if she could see his baby pictures. The only picture they could find was the one on the announcement of Bob's birth. Monica was stunned. "When I looked at it, my eye was immediately caught by his birth weight—9 pounds 11 ounces." Her new boyfriend's unlikely birth weight resonated with the message she was certain Michael sent.

Monica has come to believe in fate. Her husband Michael was killed on September 11th. Her new husband, Bob, was spared. She isn't sure what all of this means, but she has absolute faith that God has some kind of plan, even if she doesn't always understand it.

Michael and Monica

CHAPTER THREE

Going Forward with Love

Although Lisa O'Brien and Courtney Acquaviva don't know each other, they have shared similar spiritual experiences surrounding the deaths of their husbands, and they both have children who have spoken about communication with their fathers. Lisa's husband, Timmy, and mine were good friends who worked next to each other at Cantor Fitzgerald. She and Timmy lived on Long Island, and Eamon and I lived in Connecticut, but we managed to get together several times a year. I've come to know Lisa better in the last few years. Courtney's husband, Paul, worked at a different division of Cantor, and we didn't know each other. Courtney and I spoke for the first time after I started working on this project.

Lisa O'Brien, Wife of Timothy "Timmy" O'Brien

Timmy and Lisa O'Brien's wedding photograph

Lisa's story begins in the summer of 2001 when she received an unexpected visit from a neighbor who said she had something to tell her. It seems that the neighbor had recently seen a well-known local psychic/medium by the name of Tom Trotta. In the course of her reading, Trotta told her that he had a message for someone else—someone named Lisa.

M y neighbor was nervous about telling me any of this," Lisa told me. "She didn't want to give me the impression she was totally off-the-wall, but what she had heard from Tom Trotta was so convincing, she felt as though she had to tell me. My neighbor said, 'You are the only Lisa I know.'"

Both Lisa and her neighbor were surprised at the psychic's insistence. Nonetheless the conveyed message was compelling. It was also filled with accurate details. Trotta had said that Lisa's grandfather, who had died ten years before, was making himself known. Trotta was even able to describe the outfit that Lisa's grandfather was wearing when he was buried, down to his gray cardigan and the cap on his head.

Everything Trotta said rang true to Lisa, who also thought that if anyone would attempt to communicate with her from another dimension, it would be her beloved grandfather; it made sense that he would want to assure his family that he was okay. Lisa and her grandfather shared a very close bond, and he was always in her heart.

On the last day of her grandfather's life, after visiting him in the hospital, Lisa had gone out for the evening with friends. When she got home, she couldn't sleep because she couldn't stop thinking about him. She sensed that he was going to die and felt guilty that she hadn't stayed by his side. Finally, in the middle of the night, she got up and drove back to the hospital. She didn't think he wanted to be alone when he died, and she wanted to be with him. Standing by her grandfather's hospital bed, Lisa told him that she was there and that because he was in such pain, it would be okay if he let go. No more than a minute or two after she said this, Lisa's grandfather passed away.

Lisa was so impressed by the specific details in her neighbor's reading that she quickly made an appointment for herself with Tom Trotta. When she went to see him, she brought some family photographs with her. Her husband, Timmy, was in one of these pictures.

When the psychic looked at one particular photograph, he asked Lisa, "What do you want to know about this photo?"

"Oh nothing, that's my husband," Lisa replied.

"Lisa, I'm a psychic. I know you want to know something," Trotta said.

Lisa felt that she had to be honest about some of her most personal fears, and she replied, telling Trotta about her premonition. "Well, to tell you the truth, I've always had the feeling that he was going to die."

"Why do you get that?" Trotta asked her.

"I don't know," Lisa told him, "I just have this worry that he's going to leave my house and never come home."

Trotta continued to question Lisa about this feeling of hers, again asking her, "Why?"

"I don't know," she repeated. "Maybe it's because I'm married to the love of my life and I think that it's simply too good to be true. But I really always have this feeling that he is going to die and leave me."

Lisa asked Trotta please to be honest about what he saw. Finally, he reluctantly shared his impressions. He said, "Well, it's going to be quick. There will be a big bang; it will be very dark, and he will be somewhere high up."

Lisa couldn't get what the psychic told her out of her mind. When she got home, she told her husband about her fears. Timmy acted like he thought the whole thing was hilarious, particularly the part about the "big bang." Timmy loved teasing Lisa, and he did so every chance he got. He even pretended to bang his head against the wall and then staggered back, as though he was going to fall. Lisa didn't think this was all that funny. She wished that he would take her concerns more seriously. She had always been so anxious about her husband's safety that she made sure that he never left the house without kissing him and telling him that she loved him. If she forgot, she had been known to go so far as to chase his car up the street and make him stop. "If Timmy even went to the grocery store, I would worry," Lisa remembers. "When he came back, I would always breathe a sigh of relief and think, 'Thank God, it's not today.' Of course Timmy thought I was nuts."

After visiting the psychic, Lisa became even more worried. She asked Timmy to take the week that started on September 10th off from work. He said he couldn't. On Tuesday, September 11th, she begged him to stay home. Again, he said he couldn't. At that time, Lisa wasn't sure whether her fears were real or whether she was having some kind of bizarre anxiety attack.

On the morning of September 11th, Lisa was on her cell phone while driving to her gym. "I saw that I had a call coming in from Timmy, so I pushed the call waiting button, but something happened, and he wasn't there. I called him right back, but my calls wouldn't go through. When I pulled into the parking lot of the gym, my girlfriend was running out the door to meet me. She said, 'Something happened at the World Trade Center!'"

One of Lisa and Timmy's close friends is the former football star Boomer Esiason. His office was not that far from Lisa's gym. Lisa knew he would have a television, so she and her friend quickly drove to Boomer's. That's where she watched the tragedy unfold, but she couldn't quite absorb what was happening. "It all seemed unreal, and I didn't know what it meant," she said. "I just kept hoping that Timmy had made it out of the building. In the meantime, people kept calling me on my cell phone to tell me that they loved me. I wondered why that was happening. Did they know something I didn't?"

By the next day, Lisa had talked to several of the other Cantor Fitzgerald wives, who kept reminding her of the '93 bombings and how "the boys" had all made it out okay. Maybe their husbands were alive, but hospitalized or disoriented.

On the morning of September 12th, when she still had no word about her husband, like so many others who were looking for family members, a distraught Lisa headed for downtown Manhattan, where she searched the streets and hospitals, carrying Timmy's photograph.

Lisa had nowhere to turn, and she was desperate for information. She wanted to know if her husband was okay, wherever he was. Lisa remembered Tom Trotta, the psychic she had seen in August. She realized that it appeared far-fetched, but nonetheless, while she continued to search for Timmy, Lisa asked her sister to try to contact the psychic and ask for his help. When they got him on the phone, Trotta said that he would search for Timmy spiritually and get back to them. Trotta called Lisa on Thursday to say that Timmy had definitely passed on, and that he was okay and adjusting. Trotta said that when the plane hit, Timmy had been standing at the window with a fellow worker, and they were having a conversation about sports. Trotta was also able to be very specific in telling Lisa exactly what Timmy was wearing when he died. Lisa went through her husband's closet to be certain that the outfit Trotta described was missing. It was. As far as Lisa was concerned what Trotta was saying was further validated by one small detail: He told her that Timmy wasn't wearing any shoes. Timmy always took his shoes off at work and pushed them under his desk, so the scene Trotta described of a shoeless Timmy and a coworker talking about sports struck Lisa as incredibly real.

Lisa was very familiar with how Timmy behaved at work. In fact, they had met twelve years earlier when Lisa applied for her very first job at the Wall Street securities firm where Timmy would be her boss. Lisa said that all she could think about during her employment interview was Timmy. "I just looked at him," she said, "and I knew he was it. I even told my cousin Mike, who got me the interview, 'I'm going to marry that guy.'"

Lisa worked with Timmy for almost four years, during which time their relationship went through various stages, growing and deepening and evolving from friendship to love. They were married in 1994 and had three children. "Timmy was a great husband and father," Lisa said. "He was crazy, crazy, crazy about his kids. The second he was finished work, he would hurry home. All he wanted to do was be home with us."

O'Brien family photograph *(left to right)*: *(back)* John, Timmy, and Lisa; *(front)* Madeline and Jacie

Lisa has a very strong faith and spiritual identity, which helped her through the grieving process. "After Timmy died, I was crying and grieving all the time," Lisa told me. "I missed him so much! But I never really got angry. No matter how sad or desperate I felt, I never said, 'God, why did this happen?' I always believe that what happens is precisely what is supposed to happen. What happened to my husband and my friends' husbands was awful. It sucked beyond words, and I couldn't find a single human reason why this should have happened to us and our families, but I never questioned God. I really believe that there is a plan that we have no clue about. I trust that. But of course I missed Timmy so much I can't even describe it."

Within a week after 9/11, Lisa began to feel that Timmy's spirit was with her, telling her that he was okay and trying to give her strength. "Almost right away, I could feel his presence in the house. I would feel him walking up behind me, but when I turned around, nobody was there. Then, things started happening that I couldn't explain. I could sometimes hear him in our room, for example—and I knew absolutely that he was there. When I know he's near, even now, I start to get tingles on the top of my head."

A strange thing that happened all the time in the year after Timmy's death, and sometimes still happens, involves Lisa's bed. It would shake and reverberate in the middle of the night. "It felt like a diving board after someone jumps off," Lisa told me.

One night when Lisa's mother stayed over, she and Lisa both fell asleep on the bed. In the middle of the night, the bed started shaking. "Mom," Lisa said, "do you feel that?" Her mother replied, "Lisa, you're dreaming. Just go back to sleep."

The next day, Lisa overheard her mother talking to her sister, Lisa's aunt, telling her about how she too had felt the reverberating bed and that she was afraid to tell Lisa that she was right in what she was experiencing.

"Mom," Lisa said, "why did you say you didn't feel it when you did?"

"I didn't want to upset you any more than you are upset already," her mother replied.

"So you'd rather let me think that I'm crazy?" Lisa laughed.

Lisa feels that Timmy is frequently in her bedroom, communicating with her in the night, sometimes when she is asleep and dreaming, and sometimes just as she drifts off. She says that these experiences seem totally real. Timmy doesn't really talk during these communications, but Lisa is able to tell what he is feeling and thinking. When Timmy comes to her in this way, Lisa believes he is simply trying to stay close and assure her that he is still around and looking after her.

Another one of Lisa's close friends, Trevor*, was lost on 9/11. He was married to a woman named Kira*. One night Trevor also came to Lisa in her dreams. She described this event as an almost out-of-body experience and said that Trevor took her to an incredibly and indescribably beautiful garden filled with extraordinary colors and flowers. While she was there, Trevor gave Lisa a personal message that he asked her to convey to his wife.

In the light of day, Lisa was very nervous about talking to Kira. "I didn't want to upset her, and I also didn't want her to think that I was off my rocker. Finally I told her what had happened. I said, 'I don't know if this means anything, but this is what Trevor told me.' When I repeated Trevor's words, a very personal way he used to tell Kira how much he loved her, Kira's jaw dropped open."

"I've been hoping and praying to hear exactly what you told me from Trevor," Kira told Lisa.

Lisa's experiences in communicating with her husband have taken place at night; she has never actually seen Timmy when she is wide awake and moving about. However, Lisa and Timmy's youngest daughter, Jacie, who was four in September 2001, frequently saw and spoke to her father. Lisa first became aware of this one day when Jacie was in the bathroom, and Lisa asked her to turn off the light. Jacie replied, "Daddy already told me to turn it off."

"What do you mean, honey?" Lisa asked.

"Daddy said turn off the light, like a hundred times."

Not long after that Lisa heard Jacie upstairs chatting.

"Who are you talking to?" she asked.

"Daddy and the boys," Jacie replied.

"The boys" was the term that was often used to describe the group of friends who worked together at Cantor Fitzgerald.

Lisa went downstairs and got a picture of her husband and his friends from work, and she showed it to Jacie. Without hesitation, Jacie was able to tell her who was who and who was in the room with her and her daddy. "That's Eddy Schunk," she said, "and that's Tommy McHale. He laughs like a hyena." One of the men she identified was my husband, Eamon McEneaney. Lisa was floored. Her daughter was only four years old; some of the guys in the photograph she had never even met; others she had only met once or twice briefly when she was still a toddler. Yet she was able to correctly identify them by both their first and last names. That's when Lisa realized that Jacie was regularly hanging out with her father.

Not long after that, Jacie's teacher pulled Lisa aside to tell her that she saw Jacie out by the school yard swing set laughing and appearing to have conversations with invisible companions. Once again, Jacie said that she was talking to her father and the boys.

"What are you talking about?" Lisa asked her.

"They're funny," Jacie replied. "They tell me jokes." When Lisa questioned her further, she discovered that her daughter was hearing knock-knock jokes from her father and his friends.

Jacie would sometimes come into Lisa's bedroom to sleep with her mother during the night. When she did so, she told Lisa something else. "Daddy is here, too," she said. "He comes in the middle of the night and sits at the bottom of the bed. Sometimes he pats your hair and kisses you."

Other times during daylight hours, Jacie would tell Lisa that her daddy was also in the room. "What is he doing?" Lisa asked.

"He's sitting in that chair over there, and he's laughing at you," Jacie told her. "He thinks you're funny."

One day when Lisa was crying, Jacie asked her, "What's wrong, Mommy?"

Lisa told her, "I just miss your daddy so much."

"Why don't you talk to him," Jacie said. "He's right over there."

At first Lisa would sometimes get scared about some of the paranormal events taking place around her. Then she talked to a couple of people who reassured her. They told her that in all probability, it was her husband, and she didn't need to feel afraid. Nonetheless, Lisa began sleeping with a Bible by her side. She would regularly turn to Psalm Eighteen: *The Lord is my stronghold, my fortress, and my champion, my God, my rock where I find safety.* Lisa prayed that the house and the people in it would be surrounded by the white light of the

Holy Spirit. She also prayed that Timmy continue to watch over them and be with them.

Other things also happened in the house that Lisa associates with Timmy. For one thing, she would see shadows in the hallway or something moving out of the corner of her eye. Sometimes, at night, she heard knocking. It was always the same. Three loud knocks with pauses between each knock. She would look everywhere, and she couldn't find any explanation. She checked for squirrels and woodpeckers and the possibility that some other creature had gotten into the house, but there was never a reasonable explanation. Also objects, such as pictures on the wall, would move. They would fall off the wall or become very slanted. Lisa said that she would fix them and come back into the room soon thereafter, and the same thing would have happened again, and there was absolutely no reason why.

Lisa also quickly realized that lights would regularly flicker when she talked about her husband. "Timmy and I always celebrated our wedding anniversary. On the first anniversary after his death, a group of friends took me out to dinner. We were sitting at a large table. There were light sconces on the wall throughout the restaurant. Whenever we said Timmy's name, these lights near our table would flicker. This only happened to the lights near our table. A couple of my friends said, 'Seriously, Lisa, did you see that?' I told them that of course I did, but I was already accustomed to that kind of thing happening."

Lisa is also somebody who has found coins, particularly quarters, which she associates with her husband. "When Timmy and I first met, we had this thing about quarters," she recounted. "It started at work. The guys, who would sometimes get bored, were always fooling around and playing like kids. One day, somebody was singing the song 'A Penny for Your Thoughts.' In the song the singer promises a nickel for some kisses and a dime for saying 'I love you.'

"The guys began to throw coins, mostly pennies, nickels, and dimes," she rememered. "Timmy threw a quarter at me. I threw one back. This happened lots of times. We hadn't started dating yet, and we were always flirting with each other without ever admitting that we were doing it. I don't think either one of us wanted to say or do anything until we were sure how the other person felt, and also we were nervous about starting something because we were working together. Don't forget, Timmy was the boss! I remember one day after throwing a quarter at me, Timmy saying, 'Someday I'm going to cash in my quarters.' I was so pathetic, and so much in love with Timmy. Everything he touched was special to me. I took the first quarter he threw at me that way, and I taped it to a piece of cardboard with a little picture of him. I put it in my wallet and carried it around with me. Later, when we both knew we were serious about each other, he opened his desk drawer one day and showed me his quarter collection. He had kept *every* single quarter I ever threw at him.

"When Timmy finally was ready to acknowledge that we were more than just friends, he invited me to dinner. When we sat down at the restaurant he reached into his pocket, took out a quarter, and slipped it across the table to me. It was his way of letting me know that he was ready to take the relationship to a different level.

"After he died, I started finding quarters in strange places, and I could find no explanation except that somehow they were from Timmy. The first one I found was in my bed under the covers! It felt like it had to be Timmy. Why else would I have a quarter in my bed? I found them stuck behind the frames of pictures that were hung on the wall. I found them in my shoes, and I found them in my pants pocket. Finding a quarter in the pocket of your jeans may not seem unusual to most people, but I have always had a thing about not putting money in my pockets. I never do it, so if I were to take a pair of clean jeans, straight out of the dryer, and put them on and find a quarter in a pocket, it was very strange. I would vacuum the floor and then walk back over where I had just vacuumed and find a quarter."

When Lisa started to date again, she would regularly talk to Timmy, asking for his advice about the men she met. She would ask Timmy to somehow give her a sign that he was watching over her. She particularly remembers an experience with one man, who dropped by her house to visit, and for some reason she didn't hear the doorbell. Later he told her that he had been there. She had a hard time accepting his explanation. "I'm telling you," he said, "I was just there. I left a quarter on your step so you would know."

"What?" Lisa asked. "Most people leave notes. Why would you leave a quarter?"

"I don't know," he replied. "I just reached into my pocket and found a quarter. It seemed right at the time." Lisa was certain that it was Timmy's way of telling her that it was okay for her to date.

Lisa visited several psychics and mediums after her husband died, and she's received some amazing messages. She told me that she always made a point of not revealing her name or any details about her life. Once, at the last moment, a friend who couldn't attend gave Lisa tickets to a taping of the John Edward show. Edward quickly identified her as a 9/11 widow and told her that Timmy visited her regularly. He said that Timmy had been with her recently when she was at a restaurant, sitting outside. Edward correctly identified the restaurant being near where he, John Edward, lived. John Edward said that a bird had landed on her table, and that she, Lisa, had started talking to it. It was 100 percent true. Lisa was on a date. When the man had left the table for a minute, a bird flew over and perched in front of her. Lisa started talking to it, confiding her ambivalence about even being there on a date. "I knew it was crazy," she said and laughed. "But I was talking to this bird as though it was Timmy." It had happened exactly as Edward described, and exactly in the neighborhood he described.

There was another strange and unique detail that Edward brought up: A friend of Lisa's was hospitalized, and Lisa was going to visit him. The friend told Lisa that he needed a phone. Lisa remembered that there was an unused prepaid phone card among Timmy's belongings, so she picked it up and took it to her hospitalized friend. When Edward was talking to Lisa, he indicated that he was getting a message about this. "What's with the phone card?" he asked.

On at least one occasion a message that Lisa received from a medium had a practical application. In late October 2001, a medium Lisa visited told her that he saw her attending a World Series game in Arizona. Lisa repeated this to several friends, saying that there was absolutely no way that she was going to be in Arizona for a ball game. It happened that the 2001 World Series was played between the New York Yankees and the Arizona Diamondbacks. Arizona won the first two games on their home field. They then came to New York to play. One of Lisa's friends had heard enough accurate predictions from Lisa that he decided to make a bet. If Lisa was going to see a ball game in Arizona, this meant that the Diamondbacks were not going to win enough games in New York to take the series. He placed a generous bet on that. Sadly, it turned out that Lisa had to be in Arizona for the funeral of a close friend who died suddenly when his private plane crashed. While she was there, friends who had World Series tickets insisted that Lisa accompany them. Lisa went, fulfilling the psychic's predictions. When she returned home, the friend who made the bet gave her half his winnings.

Other members of Lisa's family have also visited psychics and mediums. When Lisa's sister, for example, was about to get married, she visited a psychic who told her that at her wedding she would be surrounded by deceased loved ones. The psychic told her that if she would look carefully at the wedding photographs, she might be able to see little lights representing these souls.

"My family has lost so many people in the last few years," Lisa said. "My sister dedicated a part of the wedding ceremony to these people. She mentioned everybody who had died, and it was absolutely beautiful. Later, when she got the wedding photographs back, there were at least a half a dozen pictures from this part of the service that had orbs of light all over the place, like little halos. My brother thought it was the photographer's fault, but these were professional photographers. I think it was like the psychic said: It was their way of letting us know they were at the wedding."

Within the last few years, Lisa got married again and had a new baby. Even so, she still continues to feel Timmy's presence and energy around her. Sometimes her new husband is also aware of strange things. As Lisa was talking to me, her new husband reminded her to tell me about what happened one Christmas Eve.

"We came back from a party and made sure the kids were all asleep," Lisa began. "I still hadn't wrapped all of the presents, so my husband and I were downstairs wrapping. That's when we heard the three loud distinct knocks, with pauses between each knock. There was no missing it and there was no confusing it for something else. We have a video monitor, and we could see that the baby was asleep. I thought maybe it was one of the other kids, so I told my husband to go up and be the bad guy. But when he came back downstairs, he said it was definitely not the children. They were all sound asleep. I told him, 'It's probably one of our dead guys saying hello on Christmas Eve. It's all good. Don't be afraid.'

"'How come you never get scared?' he asked me.

"'Because I'm used to it. I have always felt as though Timmy has never left me. He's always here,'" I told him.

I asked Lisa about Jacie, who has grown into a typical preteen with friends and interests. Lisa told me that she doesn't see her father anymore, but she remembers when she did.

And then Lisa told me something truly fascinating. Gwenyth, the now two-and-a-half-year-old baby girl she had with her new husband, has started seeing and talking to Timmy—much like Jacie did when she was younger. Gwenyth began by pointing at something one evening when the lights were turned off.

"What are you pointing out?" Lisa asked.

"I see Timmy," Gwenyth responded. Then she said, "I see him on your bed, Mommy, 'keesing' you and playing with your hair." Lisa is convinced Jacie didn't tell Gwenyth about her own experiences, and yet Gwenyth was experiencing the exact same thing that Jacie had!

Recently Lisa's mother was visiting. Gwenyth, pointing to Lisa's car, told her grandmother, "I want to drive Mommy's car." Gwenyth's grandmother picked her up, got into the front seat of the car with Gwenyth on her lap, letting the little girl turn the steering wheel and pretend to drive.

There was another car in the driveway, one that Timmy had given Lisa many years before. Gwenyth changed her focus to that car. "I want to drive Timmy's car," she said. Then she added, "Timmy's right there." "Where's Timmy?" Lisa asked her. "He's right there," Gwenyth said, this time pointing in the air toward the house, as if Timmy was standing right there.

Several people have reminded me that children are more spiritually attuned than adults and that it may be easier for them to get glimpses of the other side. About a month or so after I interviewed Lisa, I was visiting my hairstylist, Nicole, and I began talking about this book. She surprised me by saying that her little girl, Sheridan, regularly "sees" people who have passed away. Almost as soon as Sheridan, who is now four, learned to speak, she began to tell her mother about seeing family members who had died. It's not unusual for Sheridan to say, "Guess who visited last night?" and then start naming dead relatives. Sheridan speaks often of seeing her grandma Angela, who died when Sheridan was a year and a half old. This particular grandmother had a thick Italian accent. One day when Sheridan was about three, her mother heard Sheridan counting with an equally thick accent, "One-a, two-a, three-a." "What are you doing?" Sheridan's mother asked. "I'm counting with Grandma Angel," Sheridan replied.

When asked to describe the people she is seeing and what they are wearing, Sheridan is uncannily accurate and more often than not describes a recognizable outfit. Another grandmother, who died before Sheridan was born, usually visits wearing a red dress and carrying red flowers. This grandmother often wore red and loved red carnations. Nicole is positive there is absolutely no way her little daughter could have known any of this.

Recently an older family friend passed on. After his death, Sheridan, who called this man Poppa Tony, said that she saw "Poppa Tony playing with big dogs on Trinity Place." Nicole was stunned, because Tony used to live on a street called Trinity Place with several large dogs, something Sheridan couldn't have known. Sheridan's mother says that her daughter is uniquely in touch with her spirituality. "She loves going to Mass with me, and she's very happy about being there and sitting through the entire service. She's very inquisitive about anything spiritual and is very kind and loves to help others. If you ask her, she says, 'I'm four, but I feel a whole lot bigger than that.'"

I found myself fascinated by the notion of children receiving messages from the deceased. When I began to talk about it, another friend told me about seeing a Diane Sawyer special several years back. It was about the children born after 9/11 whose fathers perished on that date. She told me that one of the mothers said that her little son had seen his daddy. I was able to get a transcript of that show and learned that the mother's name was Courtney Acquaviva, the widow of Paul Acquaviva, who was a vice president at e-Speed, a division of Cantor Fitzgerald.

Courtney Acquaviva, Wife of Paul Acquaviva

Courtney is the mother of Sarah, who was almost three when her father died, and Paul Jr., who was born in December of 2001. Paul and Courtney met and fell in love while they were still in high school. Paul was a football player; Courtney was a varsity soccer player.

"I met Paul when I was passing under a doorway and saw him coming in the other direction," Courtney told me when describing their relationship. "Oh my gosh, he was so good-looking! I asked a girlfriend who he was, and from that minute on, I

Paul Acquaviva

don't think he had a chance. Paul and I came together as teenagers, and we never parted. From the minute we started going out, we were completely involved with each other. We were like one name—PaulandCourtney, CourtneyandPaul. We ran together; we shot baskets together; we shopped together. He helped me pick out my prom dress. The only thing he didn't help me pick out was my wedding dress because I didn't want him to see it ahead of time."

Paul and Courtney both went to college on the East Coast, and for a time, they were at the same college, Rutgers, where they even took a sports history class together and where Paul graduated Phi Beta Kappa. "We studied together for that class. I loved it, but it was frustrating for me. Paul was so smart. He could read something once and absorb it. It took me longer, but Paul was patient." Paul and Courtney got engaged and married while Paul was getting his law degree at Columbia.

Courtney says that in the days following Paul's death, several reporters and others asked her about their relationship, and she would talk about how great it was and how wonderful he was. She remembers one person saying, "Well, he couldn't have been perfect." As far as Courtney is concerned, her husband was pretty much perfect. "The most annoying thing he ever did was leave his half-used bottles of water lying around. In the larger scheme of things, this isn't a very big fault. We really enjoyed being with each other, and we loved each other. I never for a moment doubted the depth of our love. I know just how lucky I was to have known a love like this. Even knowing that it can exist is like a miracle."

In the months before 9/11, Courtney started to have some unusual experiences of a spiritual nature. There were a few things that happened in their house, for example, that Courtney couldn't logically explain. That August, while Paul was away on a business trip, Courtney woke up. In the middle of the night, she looked out of the bathroom window and saw two shadowy figures dressed all in white sitting in a neighbor's yard.

"I was shocked by what I saw," Courtney said. "The figures appeared to be hovering and looking over the yard. I remember that I didn't want to startle them by doing something like flushing the toilet. There was an incredible stillness in the air. It was as though time had stopped and I felt that I was witnessing something I shouldn't be witnessing. In my head I also wondered whether I was really seeing what I was seeing. I wondered if there was some laundry hanging there and that I simply wasn't able to see clearly. I literally wiped my eyes and looked again. I still saw the same thing. There was definitely some floating going on in my neighbor's yard. I went into my daughter's room and hid under the blankets with her, and that's where I spent the night."

The next morning, as soon as her daughter woke up, Courtney took her for a little walk so that she could take a better look at her neighbor's yard in daylight. There was no clothesline and there was no laundry. There was no white patio furniture. "There were a couple of chairs," Courtney said, "but they were wrought iron. There was nothing even remotely similar to what I had seen."

Courtney was reluctant to tell her husband what she saw, but she did. "He looked at me like I was out of my mind," Courtney said. "Paul was a very smart, realistic, and logical lawyer. There was absolutely no way he was going to buy into my telling him about apparitions. He didn't have an open mind about this kind of thing. I was probably more open than he was, but I wasn't all that open-minded either. I certainly never anticipated this kind of experience. My family is not religious and they are basically very grounded in reality, so I had no preparation for what happened. I didn't start learning about these things until after they happened in my own life. After 9/11 I read something that said these kinds of occurrences can happen to people who are about to lose someone. It said that the other side is sending you messages to prepare you. They know what's coming and are trying to help you make the connections that a closed mind might miss."

The Thursday before September 11th, Courtney experienced a real premonition while sitting by the side of a swimming pool. "Paul, our daughter Sarah, who was three, and I were in the Bahamas for a vacation. I was six months pregnant, and we thought this was probably going to be our last chance to get away for a while. It was a great vacation. At that moment, everything in our life was wonderful, and we were very, very happy. My daughter, Sarah, was at an age where she was completely enamored of her father. She was so cute; all she wanted to do was be with her daddy. I was looking forward to the birth of our son, and everything was just great.

"That day I was lying there by the pool, in the sun, kind of daydreaming, and suddenly this thought crossed my head, If Paul dies, what am I going to wear to his funeral? I remember thinking, 'Do they even make black pregnancy outfits?' I was almost in a trance and overwhelmed by a terrible moment of foreboding. I kept going over the details of his funeral, focusing on how I was going to shop for this black pregnancy dress. I must have looked upset because Paul asked, 'What are you thinking about?' Obviously it was such a horrible thought that I didn't tell him, but it was scary, and I didn't understand it. These were not the kinds of thoughts that I was accustomed to having. I should also mention that Paul had often told me that he didn't expect to grow old. He said he couldn't envision being forty and couldn't see himself at that age. When we found out that this baby was going to be a boy, Paul also said that he couldn't see himself in the future playing with a son, which at the time I thought was strange, because Paul was a great father. Now, of course, I wonder if he somehow knew on some level that he wasn't going to be here for our son's birth."

The morning of September 11th was a little bit unusual because, out of the blue, on Monday, the day before, Paul had unexpectedly been let go from his job. His department had been downsized. "We weren't really worried," Courtney said, "because he knew that he had a job waiting for him with a law firm if he wanted it. He had brought home all his personal items, like photographs from the office on Monday, so he didn't have to go back to pick anything up. He didn't have to go to work. He got a 'get out of jail free card' and he didn't take it. He could have stayed in bed for another hour or just taken his time, but he had some things he wanted to finish up. Paul always played by the rules and did the right thing, and that day, he paid for it.

"When Paul left for work, my daughter gave him two extra kisses. He sneezed, and I said, 'Bless you.' I sneezed, and he said, 'Bless you.' I remember he sighed, and I said, 'Don't worry. Everything will be okay.' He walked out the door, leaving his water bottle on the counter. I still have it. A short while later, the phone rang. My daughter was watching a video, *Barney Goes to the Zoo*. It was my brother calling. He told me about the plane hitting the World Trade Center. I told him not to worry because I didn't think Paul could have gotten there so quickly. I turned on the TV and saw the hole in the building.

"Paul always had trouble reaching me when he called from work on his cell phone, but I'm so grateful that on that morning, the phones worked. Paul called me twice. On the first call, I thought he was still on his way to work and I started to tell him about the plane. 'No,' he said. 'Listen, I'm up here. I'm going to try to get down.' I didn't hear panic in his voice or in the background. I said, 'Okay, I love you.' I called his parents. Then Paul called back, and I could now hear panic in the background. 'We're trapped,' he said. 'We're not going to get out of here. Do you know where the life insurance information is?' 'Yes,' I said. 'I know where it is. I will take care of everything.' 'I love you, Court,' he said. 'I love you, too,' I told him.

"I don't know whether we hung up or the phone went dead, but I will always be grateful that our last words were about love. I just wanted it to be about love, and that's what I wanted to carry forward. My daughter was actually making a little piece of art for her father at the time. She looked at me funny and asked, 'Is Daddy coming home?' 'No,' I told her, 'I don't think he's going to be coming home.' I kept trying to stay calm. I made a decision at that moment that I could either crumble and fall apart or I could stand up and take care of my kids. I decided that our children had to come first. That's what I did. Two days later, on Thursday, my house was insane, filled with people, and I was crazy with pain missing him. It was very hard to do, but I pulled myself together and took my daughter to the park. I vowed that there was no way that the people who caused this were going to take away my daughter's childhood. I was determined to give Paul's children—our children—a good life."

"Within the first week, I had a very intense dream that felt totally real in which Paul came to say good-bye. He was hugging me, and I said to him, 'What are we going to do now?' I was crying. He said, 'You'll do what you have always done.'"

Courtney said that the dream was different from an ordinary dream. "It was so real it was as though he was in the room. I'll never forget it. I still have very real dreams about Paul. They happen at about four in the morning. When he leaves, I wake up, shocked. I can't believe that he's not there. My mind has to catch up to reality. How could he be gone? I ask myself. He was just with me. At first, when I wake up, I'm upset that he's gone, but then I remember the connection we shared in the dream, and it brings me some peace."

Courtney has always been afraid of flying because she always had dreams about plane crashes. "Soon after 9/11, I had this vivid, vivid dream. I was in a plane with my daughter, and I was holding her tight," she told me. "The plane flew into a building, and it exploded. The building flew apart, and there was absolute carnage everywhere around me. It was a completely violent act and it was so real that I could feel the heat from the explosion. And then, almost immediately, I was floating through the air and I was surrounded by absolute and complete peace. As violent as the dream had been a second before, that's how peaceful it was as I was floating through the air. I remember thinking, 'This must be what Paul experienced.' At that moment, I was also completely serene because I knew wherever I was, Paul was also there, and I was just waiting for him. The peace was unbelievable and definitely otherworldly. I woke up, and my first thought was, WOW! Since then, I've had no fear of death. My only concern about dying is leaving my children before they are old enough to take care of themselves. I will always remember the serenity of the peaceful moment, knowing that I was just waiting for Paul."

After September 11th, Courtney's daughter also began to dream about her daddy. Courtney told me that one of Sarah's favorite activities that summer had been going to the beach with Paul and flying her Elmo kite. After her father's death, Sarah told her mother, "Daddy comes to me at night and we fly our Elmo kites." I told Courtney that I was struck by Sarah's choice of words, particularly the phrase "comes to me." It was the kind of language one might expect from a medium, not a three-year-old child. Courtney agreed, but she was positive about what her daughter said.

After 9/11, Courtney joined a support group with other women who had lost their husbands. Several of them had had spiritual experiences that made them feel that their husbands were somehow sending messages, but Courtney was still essentially skeptical. Then, one evening, her group had a gathering and invited a medium. "I was just standing there, drinking a glass of wine and eating some cheese, and I listened to this young woman do readings for some of the others," Courtney said. "She did a couple of the other women really well, and then she zeroed in on me. She started to name some people who were part of my life. She talked about seeing a Bible, and I said, 'That's not me.' But I remembered that my father-in-law was going to church quite a bit, so it was possible that he was her reference point. She described my bedroom and the shelving in it and a photo of my son on the top right-hand corner. She was accurate, but it could have been a lucky guess. I thought, 'If she is telling me something from Paul, I would expect him to speak about something that is not a lucky guess, something that I couldn't refute.' Then she started to laugh, 'Why,' she asked, 'is he showing me curtains being sewn together?'

"I think everybody in the room watched the color drain from my face. The hair on my arms stood up. There was absolutely no way she could have known anything about my curtains. After Paul died,

I decided to move to a new house. In the house I lived in with Paul, he and I had done everything together. He helped me pick fabric, curtains, furniture, even the pillows. When I was moving, I wanted to bring the best of that house and blend it into the new house. Among other things, I wanted to use the old curtains. But they didn't fit. The only way they would work on the windows was if they were sewn together. Nobody knew about this. Nobody! The medium also couldn't have known that Paul was the kind of man who helped me choose curtains. This was exactly the kind of comment that Paul knew would convince me of his presence. When I drove home that night I was shaking, and it wasn't from the wine."

When Courtney's son, Paul Jr., was about three, something else happened that she couldn't ignore. Courtney was negotiating with him about getting him his own "big boy bed" to sleep in. Paul was always a good sleeper, but as soon as he learned he could crawl out of his crib, he would do so and head for Courtney's bed or his sister's bed. When Courtney talked about getting him his own bed, he said he didn't want to be alone. One day while her son was watching a Wiggles DVD, she started talking to him. "You know," she said, "we really have to start working on your sleeping alone in your big boy bed. You used to sleep alone in your crib in your room." He replied very matter-of-factly, "But I wasn't alone."

"What do you mean?" Courtney asked, in what she hoped was a nonchalant tone.

"Daddy was in there with me," he said.

Courtney was stunned, but she continued asking her child, "What do you mean?"

"Daddy comes and sits by me at night," her son told her.

Courtney had no idea where this could be coming from. She had never told him anything like this. As far as she knew, he had never been exposed to anything that might have provided groundwork for what he was saying. She called both her parents and her in-laws to ask whether they had ever said anything like "Daddy is an angel, looking over you." They assured her they had not. Courtney said she was blown away by her son's statement.

Courtney had another surprise. After she and I spoke for the first time, she told her mother about this project. That's when her mother said, "I didn't want to upset you, but I saw Paul after he died."

Courtney was shocked. "When? And what do you mean?"

Her mother told her that a month or so after 9/11, she had gone to the park with a very pregnant Courtney and little Sarah. Courtney started playing ball with Sarah. "That's when I saw Paul," her mother said. "He was near a tree. He was smiling at you and watching you and Sarah. He was also shaking his head and laughing because you were so pregnant and trying to play basketball."

Courtney said that she couldn't believe that her mother didn't tell her anything about it at the time. I wasn't surprised that Courtney's mother hadn't said anything. I have found that many people have experiences like this, and for obvious reasons, they are reluctant to talk about them.

Courtney has come to believe that her husband, Paul, is somewhere looking over his family. "It's not like I think he's floating over my head playing a harp, but there are too many times where I have clearly felt his presence. Sometimes I'll be sitting in my backyard and there will be a small wind or breeze and I breathe it in, and something flutters in my heart, and I know he's still here for me. It gives me a great sense of peace. I'm big into energy and love. I think it's all about love and that love continues one way or another. When my son blinks a certain way, he looks exactly like his father, or when my daughter says something and I can see that she is so much like her father or when the wind blows a certain way and I feel that flutter in my heart. I don't know what it is, but I definitely believe there is more than what we experience here on earth. All I know is that you have to keep going forward with love."

Paul and Courtney Acquaviva at their wedding

CHAPTER FOUR

Many Messages, Much Inspiration

(Left to right): Welles Crowther's father, Jeff; sister, Honor; mother, Alison; and Welles

The people who knew Welles Crowther talk about his kind and generous spirit; they remember his high energy, spontaneity, and caring nature; they describe his many talents—for friendship as well as sports like lacrosse and hockey. Just about everybody has a story to tell about his kindness and compassion. His friends also talk about his unforgettable traits and preferences: They remember that he always carried a red bandana and that he considered 19, the number on his high school and college sports jerseys, to be his lucky number. Most talk about how much they admired him. Almost everybody talks about his love of life.

W elles, a twenty-four-year-old equities trader with Sandler O'Neill, found pleasure in just about everything, including working in the World Trade Center. He would call his father and ask, "Is it raining?" When his father replied "Yes," Welles got a kick out of telling him, "Not up here." Welles liked the feeling of working up high above the clouds. He also appreciated living in an apartment that had a view of the Empire State Building.

In the summer of 2001, Welles's family and friends noticed that he was acting strangely. People who knew Welles seem universally reluctant to describe his mood as "depressed" or "despondent" because that was not how Welles ever acted. As his friend and former coworker Angelo Mangia said, "Welles was always so up—always the glass is half full, never the glass is half empty." Nonetheless, Angelo remembers that Welles appeared restless and "different" that summer. He seemed somber, more serious, and Welles was never "down." In conversations with Angelo, Welles also started saying something that Angelo didn't understand. "I don't know where I'm going to be. I just know I'm going to be part of something big." He repeated this statement more than once.

In August, Welles came to talk to his father, Jeff. He told him he was thinking of leaving his job and joining the New York Fire Department. Like his father, Welles had been a volunteer firefighter in Rockland County, New York, where he grew up, so becoming a firefighter wasn't totally far-fetched. Nonetheless, as his father reminded him, a firefighter's salary was far different from the one he earned as an equities trader. But Welles said that he wanted to help people, and he thought he needed more action than he was getting at a desk in front of a computer.

Welles spent Labor Day weekend at his parents' house. "He was different—almost melancholy," his mother, Alison, told me. "Welles was a very social person. Usually when he came home for a visit, he would spend a short time with us and then he would rush off. This time, he didn't want to do anything except be with us. He spent a large amount of time going over old albums and photographs and appeared almost to be reviewing his life. Both my husband and Welles were volunteer firefighters, and we have a tradition of going to the local fire-fighters' picnic on Labor Day weekend, so we did that, but instead of grabbing a hamburger and then going off with friends, Welles hung out with us. One of those nights, there was a really beautiful moon, and I suggested driving up to a wonderful spot in a nature preserve that overlooks the Hudson to look at it. Welles said, 'What a great idea.' I remember being a little surprised. After all, what guy his age wants to take a drive with his parents to a romantic spot to look at the moon? But he wanted to be with us."

Alison certainly noticed the change in her son, but at the time she was happy to see his obvious appreciation of his relationship with his parents. She thought it was an indication of how much he had matured and grown.

Welles also brought up the idea of changing careers with his mother. She remembers telling him that his parents would support whatever he wanted. She tried to be helpful about a career change, suggesting the possibility of graduate school. At one point, while he was looking at some old photographs, "he seemed sad." Alison wondered if he was having romantic problems revolving around a new or old girlfriend, so she asked him. He said, "No, Mom, nothing like that." Shortly before he left to go back to his own apartment in NYC, Welles was looking at an old college photo. "Mom," he asked, "do I look okay in this?" That's when he repeated what he had already told his friend Angelo. "Mom, I don't know what it means. But I do know this. I'm meant to be part of something really, really big."

On Friday, September 7th, Welles exchanged e-mails with Angelo. Until recently Angelo had worked with Welles at Sandler O'Neill, but

Angelo, who lived on Long Island, was offered a job closer to his home, which he started in June. Otherwise he, too, might have been in the WTC that day. Because of his new job, Angelo hadn't seen as much of Welles that summer. Even so, he couldn't help thinking about the change in Welles's mood and was concerned enough to send Welles an e-mail, asking if he was okay. Welles answered it on Friday afternoon. This is what he said:

```
Subj: well...
Date: Fri, 7 Sep 2001 3:00:56 PM Eastern Daylight Time
From: "Welles Crowther" <wrcrowther@▮▮▮▮▮.com>
To:   ajmangia▮▮▮▮▮▮

I'm okay, but a few words come to mind...
anxious
frustrated
aimless
bored
lobster
cold beer
the coast of maine
forever
welles
out
```

Welles's e-mail to Angelo Mangia

Angelo keeps a copy of this e-mail in a credenza in his office within reach of his desk. "I've always thought of the e-mail as both poetry and a premonition," he said.

Alison remembers having a premonition of her own that summer, although she didn't initially define it as such. In July she suddenly had an unusual mental picture come into her head. It was a vision of Welles as a baby in a yellow jumper suit. He was filled with radiant light, and light emanated all around him. Alison spontaneously thought, "There's my angel in heaven." A second after she had this thought, she corrected herself. "I must mean my angel from heaven," she told herself. The vision was unusual enough that she thought she would tell Welles about it. She was worried that he might laugh at her, but he didn't. All he said was, "That's awesome, Mom."

On Sunday, September 9th, Alison and Jeff Crowther went into

NYC to have dinner with Welles and one of his friends. As they were walking down the street, Welles reached into his pocket and pulled out his wallet, a comb, and the ever present red bandana. Alison laughed. "I can't believe you are still carrying that," she said. When he was about seven, Welles had started emulating his father, who always carried a blue bandana. Welles, who never stopped looking up to his father, decided he would do the same, only his would be red. Over the years, some people teased Welles about his red bandana, but it didn't matter. "You never know when you're going to need a bandana," Welles would say. As a kid, Welles would wrap his bandana around his head, sometimes covering it with a sports helmet.

Welles, age seven, wearing his bandana

The week before September 11th, Alison had started feeling incredibly anxious; with every passing day, the anxiety became more and more intense. Alison is not normally anxious; she has never taken tranquilizers, for example, but her anxiety was deeply unsettling, and she couldn't understand it. On Monday, the tenth, Alison was at work. By the end of the day, she felt as though something was dreadfully wrong and she was unable to control the panic she was experiencing. When she got home from work, she was reeling from what she was going through. "I felt as though I was being blown apart," she said. "I felt helpless and useless and I didn't know what to do with myself. I never use the *F* word, but that night I started swearing *F* this and *F* that. I remember my daughter staring at me. Her eyes were the size of grapefruits."

Alison finally went to use her computer. "But, as I reached for my computer, it just fried. It was dead. I went to bed, but I was so anxious I couldn't fall asleep. About six A.M. I got up, got dressed, and headed for the gym." Alison was trying to process the unusual nature of what she was experiencing. "I was going over the Tappan Zee Bridge when a very clear idea came into my head. 'I know what this means,' I thought. 'I'm going to die today.' The minute I thought these words, out of nowhere a brilliant light shot out of my chest. I felt as though I was being blown out of my body. There is no way to explain what I was experiencing. It was like I was in two places. I was driving along, but I was also in this cloudy serene energy place above myself and I was completely peaceful—almost joyful. I immediately thought, 'Does this mean I'm really going to die today?' Well, I figured, if it was meant to be, it was meant to be. Anyway, it would be better than what I was going through. My next thought was that I needed to talk to a doctor. I needed some help. Why should death be better than anxiety?"

Alison managed to pull herself together and continue driving. "By this time," she told me, "I was totally objective and calm. I knew something was happening to me, but I was thinking, 'Let's see what happens.' I took a shortcut driving between two reservoirs because the water is usually peaceful and it's a lovely drive. I thought it might help me calm down." When Alison started to drive past the reservoirs, she was stunned by what she saw. "On both sides of me, coming out of the water, I saw hundreds of spiraling mists," she remembered. "The water was swirling up and going into thousands of points. I had never seen anything like this before. I remember staring at it. Then I thought,

'Well, I'm going to die anyway, so I guess I should just continue forward and see what happens.' I was remarkably peaceful." Alison understands that most people would find this experience strange and unbelievable. At the time, she certainly found it unbelievable as well.

Despite what she was going through, Alison drove on to her gym, where she worked out and showered before heading for her office, where she was preparing for a large project. Not knowing what else to do, she had decided to just go forward with her day. She was at the office when she found out what happened at the World Trade Center. Welles was able to make a call before he died. He left a message on his mother's cell phone. It said, "Hi, Mom, this is Welles. I just want you to know I'm okay." Welles did not sound frightened; he sounded very focused and as if he was moving and talking.

Like thousands of others, Alison and her husband spent the next few days calling hospitals and praying. Alison was also doing something else: She was beating herself up for not having done something to save her son. Why hadn't she been able to figure out what she was experiencing? Why hadn't she been able to do something? "I was furious at myself for not understanding the visions I had," she said. "Why wasn't I able to save anybody that day? Why was I so stupid that I couldn't save Welles?"

Nonetheless, Alison still didn't want to believe that Welles was dead, so she and her husband continued to call hospitals. Alison said, "When you called New York City hospitals that week during the day, the lines were so busy that you couldn't get through. I would start calling at midnight when there was a possibility that somebody would answer." She did this for two nights. On the third night, Alison got up at about 3:00 A.M. to stretch her legs. As she did this, she unexpectedly felt Welles there with her as a large energy field. She told me, "I could sense him. I said, 'Welles, that's you, isn't it. I guess if it's you, I can stop looking now. If you can do this, I know you are all right.' I was suddenly surrounded by this feeling of peace. I could almost hear him saying, 'It's okay, Mom—it's okay.' I didn't even want to turn my head to look to my side where I felt the energy because I didn't want to disrupt it or move it. I knew Welles was dead, and I knew I wouldn't find him in the hospital. That was my first visit with Welles."

During the next week Alison went to her church to see her minister and told him everything that had happened and what she had been feeling. She told him about her premonitions as well as her feelings of guilt and responsibility. When she told him about her vision, he said that she "wasn't meant to stop the freight train," and that "this was God's way of telling her that He would be with her." He said that what Alison had experienced was a gift from God, and he asked her if she knew what she should do with this gift? "Help people," Alison replied. "That's why I'm here, but I don't know how. I couldn't help Welles or anyone else that day."

"You don't have to become Mother Teresa," the rector told her. "You will know what to do. Your heart will tell you how."

Alison doesn't completely understand the things that happened to her before September 11th. She also feels that her experience has deeper meaning. "If someone like me can have visions like this, it means there is something more. Why should we be surprised when there is some evidence of life beyond our knowledge?" Alison told me that she has discovered that thoughts like this don't always go over well with everybody, so she is careful about discussing any of it. She is certain, however, that she continues to receive signs and messages assuring her that wherever Welles is, he is peaceful and happy. That brings her comfort. Alison told me that she has been very reluctant to talk to mediums or psychics because she worries that some of them are less than reliable or might take advantage of this kind of situation. She did speak to a woman in another part of the country, who she thought was sincere because she didn't charge 9/11 families. She told Alison many things that Alison feels were true and real.

In the months following 9/11, Alison and her husband continued to wonder about what happened to Welles. Other people who worked with him made it out of the building. What happened to Welles? They finally started to get more information as they read newspaper reports provided by survivors. In one report published in the *New York Times*, describing what happened to people who were on the seventy-eighth floor Sky Lobby of the South Tower, she read,

> *A mysterious man appeared at one point, his mouth and nose covered with a red handkerchief. He was looking for a fire extinguisher . . . he pointed to the stairs and made an announcement that saved lives: "Anyone who can walk, get up and walk now. Anyone who can perhaps help others, find someone who needs help and then head down." Another survivor said . . . she, too . . . had been steered by the man in the red bandana, hearing him call out, "This way to the stairs" . . . She soon noticed that he was carrying a woman on his back. Once they reached clearer air, he put her down and went back up.*

Alison knew immediately that the man with the red bandana was her son. One of the women he rescued, Judy Wein, told reporters, "I see this incredible hero, running back and forth and saving the day. People can live a hundred years and not have the compassion, the wherewithal to do what he did." Ling Y, another woman Welles helped, said that after her rescue she would go on the Internet to see pictures of those in the towers and cover up their noses and mouths to try to identify the man who saved her. When Alison read the story in the paper, she contacted the two women; they were able to identify Welles from photographs. Judy Wein credits Welles with saving her life and keeps a photograph of him on her mantel. When Welles's body was finally recovered on March 19, 2002, it was found alongside firefighters and emergency workers who had been running a command center in the lobby of the South Tower.

In the years since her son passed on, Alison continues to have unique and moving spiritual experiences that she associates with Welles. But she is not alone. She says she has become accustomed to having people tell her stories that usually begin with someone saying, "I don't know how to tell you this, but . . . "

I was able to contact several of the people who have had spiritual experiences surrounding Welles's death. Here are some of their stories.

Leslie Hanes

An art teacher friend of Alison's, Leslie told me that as she was driving to the Crowther house shortly after 9/11, she got this very clear message that she immediately recognized as coming from Welles. "You're going to see my mom, aren't you?" he said. "I want you to tell her that I love her." Leslie says that the voice came from somewhere outside of her head even though she didn't "hear" it in the ordinary sense. She also wasn't quite sure how she would convey this message to Alison. "How will she know it's you talking?" she asked Welles. He replied, "Remind her of the funny thing I used to wear on my head." Leslie, who hadn't known Welles as a child, assumed he was referring to some kind of hat. She finally conveyed Welles's message to his mother on the day of his memorial service.

Betty Lou and Cici

Betty Lou is a relative of Alison's. She waited several years to tell Alison that her daughter Cici had an experience with Welles after his death. Cici, a quiet young woman, was reluctant to talk to Alison because she was concerned about upsetting her. When Cici and Alison spoke, Betty Lou was there to provide support. Cici told Alison that soon after September 11th, she went down to Pier 93 in NYC. Cici had been deeply affected by September 11th. She had lost her job, and many of the elements of her life had been torn apart; she was feeling pretty devastated, depressed, and unhappy. Cici was sitting on a bench on Pier 93, thinking about all the things that had occurred, when she became aware of Welles's presence sitting next to her. She clearly heard his voice saying, "Hey, Cici, don't worry. You will be fine. Everything is going to be okay." Cici told Alison that she absolutely felt that Welles had come to sit with her and give her comfort and courage at this devastating time.

Noting the similarity between what Cici and Leslie described, Alison shared Leslie's story with Cici years later. Cici wrote back a note saying, "I experienced Welles's communication in exactly the way Leslie described . . . from 'somewhere outside her head even though she didn't hear it in the ordinary sense . . .' It is comforting to know I share such an extraordinary experience with a family friend."

John Howell

John and Welles had been roommates at college. After Welles's death, John experienced what can best be described as a visitation from his old friend. John spoke to Welles on September 11th right after the first plane hit the WTC. "I called him up and said, 'Wow, what happened? We heard it might have been a small plane,'" John told me. "Welles said, 'Yeah, I heard it, I felt it, and I have to get out of here.' I said, 'Yeah, please get out of there.' That was the last time I spoke to him. Like everyone else in the world, my friends and I were glued to the TV, trying to figure out what was going on and what happened. We all wanted to know about Welles. Did he get out? It was the big question on everybody's mind.

"I don't remember if it was one or two days after 9/11. I don't know if I fell asleep or not. But what I remember clearly is Welles standing in the doorway to my bedroom, saying, 'Hey, man, everything's going to be all right.' He was there just a second and then he said, 'I've got to go now.'"

This was an important moment for John.

"I've never had anything like that happen to me before or since, and I've thought about what happened a lot. I just remember it was really clear. Welles said, 'Everything's going to be all right,' and 'I've gotta go now.'"

"Do you remember—could you see through him? Did he look solid to you?" I asked John.

"He was standing in the hallway, and I don't remember seeing the door behind him," John replied.

John explained that he doesn't normally remember any dreams and that this experience felt very different from a dream. "I really didn't think I was asleep," he said. Nonetheless John says that the experience was so unusual that he can't help questioning himself. "I didn't know if it was just my brain creating something."

John told me that he often thinks about Welles, and when he does, a calmness comes over him. He sometimes feels as though Welles is with him, and it's a very good feeling.

Tyler Jewell

Tyler, a world-renowned snowboarder, is another of Welles's old friends and a fellow lacrosse player from Boston College. After school, Tyler took a slightly different turn from many of their friends. Instead of going into business, he devoted himself to snowboarding. Tyler remembers that, unlike many other people, Welles was always supportive of Tyler's career choice.

On September 11th, Tyler was in an airplane flying over New York City on his way to Logan. When he looked down, he could see the smoke coming out of the WTC. He had a lot of buddies working there, and he remembers worrying that everyone was all right. He was later shocked to learn that Welles had died.

Tyler, who was on the U.S. snowboarding team at the Olympics in 2006 and 2010, wore a red bandana in memory of Welles. He often thinks of his friend, particularly when he sees the number 19, the number on Welles's college lacrosse jersey, remembering when they played lacrosse together. Tyler says that although he is not religious, he does believe in God, even though he doesn't picture him as a guy with a beard. Tyler says he tries to stay open to spiritual possibilities. Tyler has had one experience that he can't explain or understand. It happened when he was on a ski lift in Chile. The lift happened to be going up a mountain that was used by local people as a religious site.

"I got to a specific spot on the mountain," Tyler said, "and I started thinking about Welles. Suddenly, it was as though he was there. I didn't see him or anything, but for a minute, he was *there* next to me on the ski lift and I started having this silent conversation with him. It wasn't in my head, but it was also not like I was hearing voices. It was as though it was outside my head, but it was silent." Tyler said that it's hard to describe because this kind of thing had never happened to him before, but he felt it was definitely not taking place in his own head. Tyler said that Welles said something that was typical Welles, and Tyler was sure of Welles's presence. It brought a smile to Tyler's face.

Then, just as suddenly as it happened, the connection broke. Tyler thought, "Wow, that was weird," and he put the experience out of his mind. Tyler is very much not the kind of person who dabbles in the paranormal, and this was just too strange for him to give it much credence. Tyler made the run down the mountain, and then he got on the chair lift again. At the exact same spot, on his way up the mountain, the very same thing happened. Once again, it suddenly felt as though Welles was there. Only this time, it felt more serious, and this time, Welles had a specific message. "Listen, do me a favor," he said. "Tell my parents that I'm okay."

Tyler didn't know what to do. He knew Welles's parents and knew what a close relationship they had had with their son. He remembered that Welles's father went to every single one of his lacrosse games. He wanted to give them Welles's message, but he couldn't figure out how he could go to them and say that Welles had asked him to convey a message. It was too strange, and he worried that it might be more upsetting than not. He had no way to prove what had happened. He did tell Alison that he had been on a ski lift and that he'd felt Welles's presence, but nothing more.

Chuck Platz

Chuck met Welles in Madrid, Spain, in 1998 when both were involved with work-study programs. They became close friends and traveling companions and talked often about starting a business that would utilize their shared love of Spain. In 2000 Chuck and Welles were both in New York. Sharing an apartment and the expenses that went along with it seemed like a good move. They signed a lease and moved into their new space in September of 2000. Welles was thrilled that the apartment number at the new address was 19.

"Welles was always in good spirits," Chuck told me. "He was a great guy. We are exactly the same age, but in some ways I felt about him as if he was a big brother. Even though we were roommates, we didn't always see that much of each other. I was working really long hours, but sometimes we'd go down to our favorite local bar and reminisce about Spain; we'd talk about starting a business, and getting back there.

"On Monday night, September 10th, we watched *Monday Night Football* with another friend. I was kind of tired and went to bed early. I remember lying there in bed hearing the game in the next room." The following morning for most New Yorkers life changed dramatically. Thinking back, Chuck said, "I've been very fortunate. Not that many people in my life have passed away. Sometimes I feel as if it still hasn't totally hit me that this great man who I looked up to is gone. It's surreal. Sometimes when I think about him, I get choked up, and I'm not an emotional person."

Within a couple of months after Welles's death, Chuck had an experience that he will never put out of his mind. "The apartment we shared was in an old prewar building, and you tend to hear noises," he remembered. "You can hear footsteps in the hall and people putting keys into their locks and walking into their apartments. Living alone the first couple of months after September 11th, I would always hear keys, and the thought "Welles must be home" would cross my mind, and I would quickly remind myself that Welles would never be coming home.

"One night I was on the couch watching TV. I was dozing just a little, but I heard the key in the lock and I thought it was coming from a neighbor's apartment. Then I heard footsteps walking down my apartment hallway. That's when I realized it probably wasn't just a neighbor. I looked up and I saw Welles. He had on a dark overcoat, a suit, polished shoes. He walked in like he always did. We had a little table where we always put our keys when we came in. He stopped there. He looked at me. I was kind of sitting up, against the arm of the couch, wide eyed, and I remember gasping. I remember him saying, 'Chuck, it's okay. I'm okay.' I don't remember what happened next. I don't remember if I blinked or if he just went away."

If this was a dream, it was like no other dream he'd ever had. "First of all I don't dream very much," Chuck said. "When I do, my dreams aren't realistic. If this was in fact a dream, it was completely realistic. I was wearing exactly what I was wearing; the television was playing exactly what it was playing. Everything was exactly as it is, and there was no break between sleeping and waking . . . between what happened and what was going on around me. It was all of a piece."

Chuck told me that although he thinks about this experience often, he isn't sure if he ever told anybody about it. He doesn't think so. "It's not something I would bring up in conversation, although I certainly talk about Welles. I tell my stories about traveling around Spain together, and I wear a metal bracelet that has his name on it—it's one of my most cherished possessions—but I don't talk about this."

"I was initially shocked," Chuck said after I asked him how he felt about the experience of seeing Welles. "Then I felt this peaceful feeling—I guess that's the best way to describe it. I remember it so clearly—him walking in and pausing near the table, as if he was coming home. Then instead of walking toward his room, he paused and looked at me. I remember the look on his face. I was happy to see him, and I was peaceful. Of course there was also this sadness and feeling, I really miss this person, and I want to make sure he's okay."

Alison, Welles's mother, sometimes sends notes and messages to Welles's friends. Chuck said that he received one from her that she had received from someone else. It said, "Welles is with people who love him, who are familiar to him. He is readjusting to life as a spirit." Chuck said that these sentences from Alison jumped out at him.

"It's almost as if we go back to what we originally were," he said. "This life is temporary and we go back to a life we had as spirit and energy before this life on earth. I thought about it. One day, when I die, I will go back to a life that I will remember—a time when I was pure spirit, pure energy. I will reconnect with friends and family who have passed on. It's almost been a comforting feeling. Death is scary to just about everybody. I always had some fear of the unknown. I think that I am more at peace now with the fear of dying. Something tells me that one of the first spirits I will meet is Welles to make sure I'm okay."

In 2004, Welles's sister, Honor, gave birth to a little girl. Alison said that she couldn't help herself. She kept praying to God and talking to Welles. She was asking Welles to be present for this birth, and she was asking for a sign that he was there. As they were stitching her daughter up, they started counting sponges. The doctor kept saying nineteen, nineteen, nineteen. They had used twenty sponges, and they could only find nineteen. Finally they found the last sponge, but hearing the number nineteen again and again gave her pause. Was it a "sign"? Alison and her daughter were laughing about this in the recovery room, talking about how silly they were being, but then the first nurse that walked into the room was wearing a red bandana.

In 2006, The NYC Fire Department awarded Welles Crowther, "The Man in the Red Bandana," a special commendation:

NYC FIRE COMMISSIONER

SPECIAL COMMENDATION

Certificate of Appointment

Posthumously Awarded

WELLES CROWTHER

HONORARY FDNY FIREFIGHTER

FOR BRAVERY AND COURAGE

WHILE AIDING TRAPPED VICTIMS

During the

SEPTEMBER 11, 2001

WORLD TRADE CENTER ATTACK

KNOWN AFFECTIONATELY AS

"THE MAN IN THE RED BANDANA"

HIS HEROIC EFFORTS SAVED AT LEAST FIVE LIVES
THAT DAY.

DIRECTING PEOPLE TO SAFETY FROM THE SOUTH
TOWER'S 78th FLOOR, WELLES SACRIFICED
HIS OWN LIFE TO SAVE OTHERS.

*"People can live 100 years and not have the compassion
or the wherewithal to do what he did."*

—Judy Wein, rescued by Welles

THE OFFICERS AND MEMBERS OF
THE NEW YORK CITY FIRE DEPARTMENT

ARE PROUD TO CALL WELLES CROWTHER "BROTHER."

December 15, 2006

Hereby Given This Date

Salvatore J. Cassano   Nicholas Scopetta
Chief of Department   *Fire Commissioner*

Welles in his Boston College lacrosse uniform

Welles in volunteer firefighter uniform

CHAPTER FIVE

Finding a More Spiritual Perspective

Ruth, Juliana, and David McCourt

Men and women who have received after-death messages from loved ones often say that these communications have opened the way to personal and spiritual transformation. This is what happened to David McCourt, a deeply thoughtful man, who lost his wife, Ruth, and his four-year-old daughter, Juliana.

Ruth and Juliana were on United Airlines Flight 175, which crashed into the South Tower at the World Trade Center. They were on a trip to California in which they planned to do several things, including a visit to Disneyland and a stay at the Deepak Chopra Center. Ruth's best friend,

Paige, who was traveling to California with them, decided to use frequent
flyer miles and ended up on another flight. She was on hijacked Ameri-
can Airlines Flight 11, which hit the North Tower.

R uth and I were married for seven years," David began. "I knew
I wanted to marry her from the very first moment we met. I
proposed to her on our third date over caviar and champagne
at Petrosian's in New York City. We were married at the Vatican, and a
few years later, our daughter, Juliana, was born.

"In the early summer of 2001, I noticed that Ruth had become
somewhat distant. I asked her about it. I remember saying, 'Ruth, I feel
as though you are distancing yourself from me. Do you want out of this
relationship?'

"Ruth told me, 'I love you. This isn't about you. I'm just feeling a
lot of things right now.' I told her that I was always there for her. Soon
after that when we were sitting, looking out at the water, Ruth turned
to me. 'David,' she said, 'if anything happens to me, put my ashes
in Ireland. I want my ashes in Ireland. I also want our wills to be in
order—I would like to see the formal drafts.'

"After Ruth died, I discovered that in August, she told several
people that she felt that something catastrophic was about to happen.
She told her brother, and in August, she gave a eulogy at the funeral of
a friend of hers named June. After the service, talking to friends, Ruth
said, 'This is a tragedy, but this is nothing like the tragedy that is about
to happen.'" Paige Hackel and another friend, Sonia Puopolo, who
were standing with her, both agreed that they, too, felt a sense of foreboding. (Neither Ruth nor Paige had any way of knowing that Sonia
was also scheduled to fly to California on American Airlines Flight 11
and would meet a similar fate.)

Less than a week before September 11th, Ruth told David that she had decided to go to California with her friend Paige, and she was going to take Juliana with them. Ruth and Juliana spent the evening of September 10th at Paige's house so they could be closer to the Boston airport. That evening, David called Ruth to say good-bye. Ruth put their daughter on the phone. "Daddy, I'll miss you, and I love you," Juliana said. "Take good care of Phoebe." (Phoebe was Juliana's little dog.)

David asked Juliana to please put Mommy back on the phone. "When Ruth got on, I told her to have a good trip," David said. "Ruth told me that she would call me evening from California. We said good-bye and I started to put the phone down. Then an amazing thing happened: I saw a crash, like a big light going off in my head. It was so monumental that I had to sit down. I was stunned and silent and frozen for about thirty seconds. I remember saying to myself, 'My God, what was that?' Then a feeling of tranquillity came over me. I felt almost euphoric, and again, my feelings didn't match what was going on in my head. I was debating whether to call Ruth back, and I was walking around the room, and I was experiencing a feeling of total composure, a feeling of comfort. So I just went on with what I was doing. The rest is history.

"After 9/11, I didn't want to live. Ruth was dead. Juliana was dead. Juliana was attached to my soul, and I felt like my soul was being torn apart. I told people that losing Ruth was like having my heart ripped out, but losing Juliana was like losing my soul. I didn't want to go on, and I didn't know how I could go on.

"Ruth had left a book on my nightstand for me to read, *How to Know God* by Deepak Chopra. I started reading it, and it really gave me some hope. I very much wanted to meet Deepak and started trying to find a way to reach him. Then, at the same time, I came across a book written by Raymond Moody about near-death experiences. Moody talked to a large number of people who had died and were revived. They all talked about seeing this light, and at first, Moody attributed it to some kind of malfunction in brain-imaging. Yet he researched a few patients who went brain dead and were able to come back and related their experience. Not only that, they related what happened while they were on the operating table. They were able to repeat conversations that really happened in the room. From this, Moody knew that there had to be another dimension, because otherwise they couldn't have come up with so much specific information."

David was so impressed by what he read that he started trying to contact Moody through his publisher, something he finally did toward the end of October. This phone call was a life-changing event in David's life, and he still remembers what Moody told him. "David, all these people say the same thing," he said. "They say (a) prayer works, and (b) the main thing is feeling love and compassion toward your fellow man. Nothing else really matters." David told Moody that he didn't really believe in prayer, but Moody reiterated the same thought. "David, trust me. Everyone who comes back says the same thing. Prayer works." David listened and paid attention to what Moody told him, even though he wasn't sure it could help him. "That night I got on my hands and knees and I just surrendered," David recounted. "It wasn't a regular prayer. It was opening your heart to a God—a force. I said, 'God, Ruth, and Juliana, if you hear me . . . If you prove to me that you're on the other side, I can go on. Please prove this to me.' I woke up the next morning, and nothing had apparently changed, but what happened in the next forty-eight hours totally changed my mind."

The following day David had to be in New York City because he had a meeting with the former New York governor Mario Cuomo and his wife, Matilda. David, who wanted to do something to honor his daughter's memory, had started a foundation in Juliana's name. When David thought about Juliana, he knew that she had been raised with love and peace. These were important values, and David wanted to help others learn to resolve conflicts peacefully. He decided to help fund organizations that taught nonviolent conflict resolution, and the Cuomos had similar interests. David had already met Mrs. Cuomo, but this time she told David that she had a friend she wanted David to meet. His name was Sam*; she was seeing him the next day for breakfast and she suggested that David join them. When David asked her why she thought he should meet Sam, all she said was, "I don't know. I just feel you should—just trust me."

So the next day, David found himself having breakfast with Sam. When Sam asked David how he was doing, David honestly replied, "Not so well." David told Sam that he had been finding comfort in a book by Deepak Chopra, whom he hoped to meet. Sam immediately reached for his cell phone and, within seconds, was talking to someone, asking, "Is Deepak there?" It turned out that Sam and Chopra were good friends, and Sam quickly arranged a phone meeting.

Later that day, David McCourt answered the ringing phone in his hotel room. "Are you Dave McCourt?" Deepak Chopra asked.

"Yes," David answered.

"Are you aware that I have been desperately trying to locate you for the past eight hours?" Chopra continued.

"Why have you been looking for me?" David wanted to know.

"I just dedicated my last book, *Recovering from Fear and Suffering*, to Ruth, Paige, and Juliana. I've been reading about them, and I saw their story on TV. You know they were on their way to my center."

David was amazed to learn that while he was trying to find Deepak that morning, Deepak had asked Carol, his secretary, to try to locate David. "Find out whether Ruth McCourt has a husband," he had told her. "I've got to meet him."

"So there we were in time and space," David said. "He's desperately looking for me, and I'm desperately looking for him."

About a half an hour after he hung up, David received a call from Lorraine, a friend of Ruth's. She also had a message for David. She had spoken to a recently widowed friend of hers who received a great deal of comfort and support from a psychic medium she had visited. Lorraine had the phone number of the psychic in case David wanted to give her a call.

At first David told her, "I don't believe in those things."

But David, remembering that he had asked for "proof," decided that he had nothing to lose by calling this medium, who lived near New Haven. Because David didn't want the psychic, whose name was Marti, to know anything about him, he went so far as to borrow another person's cell phone when he called her. When David called Marti, he left a message on her machine that said, "My name is Dave. I live in NYC. I lost someone on 9/11, and I'm in a lot of pain. I'd like to talk to you."

David told me that there was absolutely no way that Marti could know who he was or anything about him. "Remember, three thousand people died," he said. "I could be connected to any of them." He told me that he didn't use his last name, nor give any identifying details about his situation. David, who lives in Connecticut, even made a point of being misleading about where he lived. When Marti called back it was to the borrowed cell phone.

"I'm so sorry you lost someone," Marti told him. "God took the best of us on that particular day, but all I can tell you is that they are in a very special place right now."

"I wish I could believe you," David replied, "but I'm struggling with this."

"David," Marti said, "I'm sure I can help you, but I have a full schedule and I'm traveling, so I can't see you for three months. Do you want to set something up for January?"

"Oh God, I don't know if I can wait that long."

"Well," Marti said, "if something comes up, I'll try to fit you in."

A disappointed David was ready to hang up, but Marti continued talking.

"Let me ask you a question," Marti said. "Ever since you called and left a message, a strong spirit has been in my house, and it won't go away. Do you know anyone who died named John?"

"No," David said.

"Are you absolutely sure?" Marti asked again, "because there is a John here who I feel is connected to you somehow."

"No," David told her again, "absolutely not."

"He keeps holding up a football," Marti continued.

Suddenly, everything changed for David, who felt chills going up and down his body. "When Marti asked me if I knew anybody named John," he told me, "I was thinking of people who had died recently. I didn't even connect to my brother John. He died while he was playing football some years ago."

The circumstances were such that Marti decided to rearrange her schedule so she could see David the following morning. David brought Ruth's friend Lorraine with him to the appointment.

"When we sat down," David said, "we talked generally for about ten minutes, and then she was quiet. 'David,' she said, 'there is a woman in this room with red hair and blue eyes. She says she loves you.' She was silent for about another forty-five seconds. Then she turned, and I'll never forget what happened next. She had tears in her eyes, and she said, 'Oh my God, you lost your little girl. She's saying Daddy, Daddy, that book you found on the floor the other night. I left that for you on the library floor.'"

David said he was stunned by this. The night before he came to New York, he had found Juliana's favorite Scooby-Doo book on the floor as Marti described. He had picked it up and put it back on a shelf in her bedroom. Marti continued the reading, telling David what she was getting from Juliana, who assured her father, "We are here and we love you, and we're okay." Then Marti got a message from Ruth, who said, "David, I don't want statues of me in Connecticut. If you are going to put up statues, do it in Ireland, not here." David had no plans concerning statues and didn't know what Ruth was talking about. As he was to discover, Ruth had several other confusing messages that she wanted Marti to convey.

"David," Marti told him, "Ruth says that she left a blinking light for you at home. If you want proof that she is here, pay attention to the wallet. She left you something very important in her wallet."

David was sure that Ruth had taken her wallet with her, and he didn't know what to make of these messages. "Do you know what she is talking about?" he asked Marti.

Marti indicated that she didn't have any idea what Ruth meant, but Ruth had more to say on other topics, particularly on how David wasn't taking good care of himself. "All you're doing," Marti conveyed, "is coming home at night and eating peanut butter sandwiches. You're living in darkness . . . you're not even turning the lights on."

"That was so true," David told me.

Then suddenly Marti had another message for David, but this time from another person. "David," Marti said, "your mother is here. Why is she calling you David Jerome? And who is Arthur? And who is Gertrude? They are here to support you."

Once again, David couldn't believe the level of specificity that Marti was able to achieve: His mother often called him by his full name, David Jerome, when she wanted to tease him. Arthur was his grandfather's name; Gertrude was his grandmother. There was no way Marti could have had this information.

One of David's most heartbreaking concerns was that Ruth and Juliana had experienced great pain when they died, but Marti assured him that this wasn't the case. Marti said that David's brother, John, had been there to help take them into the light.

David firmly believes that there were several things that Marti conveyed that no one could have known, even if they had been able to research his life. Juliana, for example, talked about the electric garage door openers at their house. David said that nobody could have known about his daughter's fascination with the device and how he would let her play with it, opening and shutting the doors. Marti also said that Ruth reminded him of what had happened a few nights earlier when he had been crying and prayed, "Ruth, if you are here, please hold my hand." Marti said that Ruth heard his request to hold his hand and that she had been there, accurately describing where his hand had been and details about how the European mattress on his bed over-lapped the box spring.

Marti also said that Ruth knew David was praying for her as well as Juliana in Juliana's room. According to Marti, Ruth said, "David, know that when you go into Juliana's room to pray, I am there. I don't bring Juliana because you are in too much pain right now." Then Ruth said something else. "And, David," she said, "please don't say that our lives were a waste."

At this moment, Marti looked at David: "You are saying that their lives were a waste?"

David acknowledged that he had indeed used that term, even though it wasn't exactly what he meant. According to Marti, Ruth added, "It was not a waste, and it was predetermined." Then, once again, Marti changed the subject. "Who is Deepak?" she asked before continuing. "Ruth says to tell Deepak that she is honored that he dedi-cated a book to her and Juliana."

At this moment, David froze. He had only learned about the dedication twenty-four hours earlier, and he hadn't told anyone, even Lorraine, who had accompanied him to Marti's reading. There was absolutely no way that Marti could have known any of this.

As Marti continued, she also had a message for Lorraine. "Who is June?" she asked. David told her that June was a close friend of Ruth's who had died earlier that year. Marti then turned to Lorraine and said, "Shopping, shopping, shopping." It was true. Lorraine and June went shopping together all the time. "Lorraine," Marti said, "Ruth says to thank you for being such a good friend and she wants you to know that she will be there for your fiftieth birthday."

"Lorraine looked at me with total incredulity," David said. "She was going to celebrate her birthday in one week, which I didn't even know."

When David returned home that evening, he first called Ruth's mother, Paula, to ask if she knew anything about any plans for a statue of Ruth.

"Yes," he was told. Paula's garden club had decided to put statues of Ruth and Juliana in a memorial garden. David explained to Paula, "Ruth doesn't want them."

Then David looked all over the house to try to find the blinking light that Ruth said she had left for him. Finally he ran down to his workout room. There, on a piece of exercise equipment, was a clock with a blinking light flashing at him. It was flashing the exact time of Ruth and Juliana's flight.

David later asked Marti about the blinking light. "I've seen this time and time again," she replied. "When spirits come through they are frequently able to use electricity to let us know that they are there." Deepak Chopra also told him that everything is energy. Spirits are operating in a dimension where their frequency is close to the speed of light. We can't see their energy, but they can sometimes slow it down to the frequency of electricity and cause things like static and flickering lights.

The other message that David couldn't understand involved Ruth's wallet. David was positive that Ruth had her wallet with her and, logically, assumed that it had been destroyed in the plane crash and fire that destroyed the World Trade Center. It would be a while before he had any idea what the message about Ruth's wallet meant. Some months later Ruth's wallet was recovered, intact, from the site at Ground Zero. Inside the wallet was a papal coin that the pope had given Ruth at the Vatican. David now carries it with him.

In the last few years, David has gone back to Marti several times for additional readings. She continues to tell him things that no one could have known. The most important thing, however, to emerge from all his experiences is his new belief that there is, indeed, another and higher dimension. Motivated by this learning, he has written a book about it called *In the Light*. "I had to experience proof," he said, "before I would believe." He views this realization as a "gift." David always tried to be a good and compassionate person, concerned with ethics and sound moral judgment, but his recent experiences have placed him firmly on a deeper, more profound, spiritual path. Dave prayed that he would be "shown" that his wife and daughter were somewhere safe and that there was "more" than this lifetime. When his prayers were answered he traveled the distance from nonbeliever to fully engaged spiritual seeker.

Juliana and David McCourt

PART THREE

GLIMPSES OF A DEEPER REALITY

Coincidence is God's way of remaining anonymous.

—ALBERT EINSTEIN

Many, if not all, of us have had spiritual experiences that we can't explain. Frequently these events are very mundane. We dream about getting a flat tire; within the next week it happens. We suddenly remember a friend we haven't spoken to in a while; within moments, the phone rings and the friend is there, saying, "Hi." Sometimes these events appear much more profound. We dream, find, see, hear, smell, or generally sense something that we can't explain. One woman has a dream in which she sees her sister standing in a doorway leading to a space where her deceased parents appear to be waiting. She gets the sense that her sister is saying good-bye to her. The dream is deeply unsettling. She wakes and thinks, "Wow, that was strange!" Two days later, her healthy-looking sister collapses and dies on her way to work. A grieving father reluctantly visits a psychic, who gives him a series of accurate messages from his late son; they have the ring of truth and he feels comforted. A daughter remembers sitting and crying after her mother's death and hearing a ringing phone. When she picks it up a woman's voice quickly asks, "Are you all right?" Then, just as suddenly, the phone connection is broken.

All of these people have been fortunate enough to have had a brief glimpse of another, deeper reality.

CHAPTER SIX

Premonitions:
Warnings from the Universe?

Thinking about my husband's many accurate premonitions started me on a spiritual quest. For many people associated with 9/11, the first spiritual messages they received came in the form of premonitions. History has been recording premonitions, heeded and ignored, since the beginning of time. We remember the biblical prophets and the cautionary advice received by Julius Caesar concerning his assassination. Caesar ignored the warnings of the soothsayer who told him to "Beware the Ides of March" as well as those of his wife, who, the night before he was killed, dreamed that he was lying dead in a pool of blood. Some of us remember reading about Abraham Lincoln's dream days before he died in which he saw a body lying in state in the East Room of the White House. Lincoln told several people about this dream, and he also wrote it down in his journal.

"Before me was a catafalque, on which rested a corpse wrapped in funeral vestments. Around it were stationed soldiers who were acting as guards, and there were a throng of people, some gazing mournfully upon the corpse, whose face was covered, others were weeping pitifully. 'Who is dead in the White House?' I demanded of one of the soldiers. 'The President,' was his answer. 'He was killed by an assassin.' Then came a loud burst of grief from the crowd which awoke me from my dream. I slept no more that night, and although it was only a dream, I have been strangely annoyed by it ever since."

What about premonitions such as these? Is it possible that the ability to anticipate tragic events before they occur is a matter of science? Do premonitions, for example, stem from a part of the human brain that we don't yet understand? Or is this all part of some higher form of communication with the divine? Are certain individuals truly selected as mediums through whom direct warnings or advisories are channeled? Nobody can deny the many reliable instances of premonitions recorded throughout history. Even so, there doesn't seem to be any acceptable scientific explanation. As one might expect, there are a variety of different explanations sometimes used by psychics and members of the New Age community.

Tom Trotta, a psychic medium, was consulted by several people whose lives were impacted by 9/11. His clients typically believe he has a high batting average for accuracy. When I interviewed him, he said that people who have premonitions or precognition are somehow able to access the Akashic Records, which are described by various mediums and psychics as a kind of universal memory or filing system. Some people even refer to the records as God's Mind. Those who accept this explanation believe that all the words, thoughts, and events that have ever happened or are likely to happen are encoded within this mystical library. On occasion, people who are sleeping, meditating, or in altered states of consciousness are somehow able to get a glimpse of small bits of this information. It's an intriguing explanation.

An unusually large number of the people I've interviewed spoke about the feelings of impending doom that either they or someone who perished experienced pre-9/11. They describe changes in behavior or conversations in which their loved ones actually said things that implied some foreknowledge of events to come; they remember spouses who suddenly wanted to clear up loose ends. Eamon purchased life insurance for the first time in the summer of 2001. Shortly before 9/11, he called me from work to ask me if he should increase the amount. I told him, "No, don't be ridiculous. Nothing's going to happen to you." I've lost track of the number of other people who told me about newly purchased life insurance policies.

Alessandra Benedetti, whose husband, Paul, worked in the World Trade Center at Aon Corporation, said that Paul suddenly became very concerned that his family would be secure in the event of his death.

Paul and Alessandra Benedetti at Windows on the World, North Tower, WTC

Although he was only thirty-two, still a young man, and they had no children, in the week before 9/11 he finished the paperwork necessary to get life insurance policies naming both his wife and his mother as beneficiaries.

Several people talked to me about having a lifetime of unusually strong worries concerning a specific loved one who perished. Paul Benedetti's mother, Sofi, said that she was always unusually anxious about her son's safety. She saw him as her "gift" and had a feeling that he was "on loan" to her for only a short period of time. She would pray regularly, saying, "I don't know how long I'm supposed to have him, but when I'm not there hovering around, taking care of him, I put him in your hands, Lord." In the year before his death, both Sofi and Alessandra remember Paul frequently saying, "Everything in my life is so perfect, I could die right now a happy man."

Premonitions are regularly experienced by ordinary people who have no claim to special gifts of ESP or paranormal abilities. Frequently, these premonitions come in the form of very realistic or even symbol-filled dreams. Other times, they are simply unexplained feelings of fear or impending doom that arise someplace in the gut. Some of the people who had the strongest sense of foreboding about 9/11 now see their premonitions as being an introduction to a variety of other spiritual experiences associated with the tragedy. Here is a sampling of some of the experiences people shared with me.

PRECOGNITIVE DREAMS AND UNEASY FEELINGS

Lorraine, Wife of Bill

Lorraine and her husband, Bill, lived in the Midwest. On September 11th, Bill, who worked for Marsh & McLennan, was at the World Trade Center for meetings. Lorraine has had several experiences of a spiritual nature including an intense dream that carried a strong premonition. She also now feels that her husband's behavior in the week before his death indicated that he also had a subliminal awareness of the future and was going through some form of spiritual transformation.

"My dream took place during the first week of September," Lorraine began. "My husband and I were both sound asleep in our bedroom along with our two dogs and one cat. It was the middle of the night. In the dream, I was standing looking at a group of people walking past me. Their left profiles were toward me, and there was no color in the dream. It was just in black, white, and gray, and it was all in slow motion. There were so many people, and they were all dressed in business attire, just walking.

"All of a sudden in the line in front of me is my husband, Bill, and I'm looking at him. I didn't call out. I was thinking, 'What's he doing with this crowd?' He was just walking along, and all of a sudden the person right behind Bill turned and looked straight at me. I can still see this man in my mind: He had very dark hair and dark eyes, dark eyebrows and lashes, but his eyes were really bright and crystalline. When he opened his mouth to speak, his teeth were like neon electric lights. His skin was also like light, and he was just beautiful. I remember he had on a dark topcoat and necktie and white shirt, but he was just like this gorgeous man. He looked like he was in his midthirties, and he turned and looked straight at me. Then he picked his right hand up and put it up over Bill's head. Bill was in front of him, and he was facing Bill's back. He used his pointer finger and kept pointing at Bill's head. Then he looked at me and whispered, as if no one in the world was supposed to hear him except me, 'He's next.' And I woke up.

"I shot right up in bed and opened my eyes," Lorraine continued. "The dream was so real I thought the man was going to be standing in front of me in my bedroom. I was in a cold sweat. I looked around the room. There was Bill, sleeping soundly next to me. The dogs were sleeping. The cat was asleep. I felt as though I had just run a marathon. I had to get out of bed and walk around.

"I was very shaken. For the next few days I couldn't get the dream out of my head. I was in a fog. I couldn't concentrate, but I didn't burden anybody with this. I didn't tell my husband because I was sure he would say something like, 'What did we have for dinner that night? Tacos?'"

About two or three days after the dream, Lorraine remembers standing at her kitchen window and looking up at a beautiful blue-sky morning, "Dear God in heaven. Please don't take him. I can't live without this man," she said. "I waited a few seconds to hear that Big Voice talking, but He said nothing and then it occurred to me, 'This is ridiculous. It was just a silly dream," I said to myself. "You're allowing it to consume your waking hours and you're having a hard time sleeping. Let it go this minute!' And I did. I just let it go."

Lorraine says it's hard to believe that she talked herself into believing it was just a dream and then ten days later her husband was gone.

She remembers many details from the final weekend that she spent with her husband. His behavior and attitude were very different from what they normally were. Her husband was usually more of an intense type A personality, but for the week or so before he died, he was incredibly mellow and calm. That Sunday, he went out to cut the grass, expecting to use his riding mower, but it wouldn't start, so he had to use a regular lawn mower, which took a lot of time. Normally he would have been annoyed. That day he was blasé and calm. "No big deal," he said. Lorraine wasn't accustomed to a husband whose default position was set at "transcendence." She told me that she made mental notes of it, watching the way he was thinking and handling things. "Wow," she thought, "who is this man?"

Lorraine will never forget something Bill told her that weekend. "If I don't have another thing in my life, I'm happy," he said. "I'm happy with my job. I'm the best at what I do. I'm happy with my children. I'm happy with the house. I love the town we live in, and if I never have another thing in my life, I'm just happy with where I'm at."

"Most people are always saying I need to achieve more," Lorraine said, thinking about her husband's words. "They want, want, want. But Bill said, 'I'm a really happy man. I don't need any more than what I have.' When he said those words to me, it was like he was holy. I felt like I was being touched by a saint, and Bill was not a saint. He was just a regular guy, and I loved him tremendously. But to hear him talk like that was almost surreal. He's not the kind of person who would delve into dreams or something spiritual. He was just a real level-headed, feet-on-the-ground kind of a guy."

As far as Lorraine was concerned, his talking like this was totally out of character.

Ellen G.*, Wife of Robert G.*

I spoke at some length with Ellen G., whose husband, Robert, died on the top floor of the North Tower. Robert loved his beautiful office overlooking Long Island, but Ellen didn't like the building and never wanted him to work there. I didn't meet Ellen until 2007 and was fortunate enough to be able to interview her in the comfortable apartment she and Robert had shared and where she was still living. It was quickly apparent that the couple had an exceptionally strong and happy marriage. They loved being together, and they loved doing things together. When I listened to Ellen talking about her husband and looked at the photographs she showed me, I wished that I had been able to meet him and know them both. Ellen described a dream Robert had in the summer of 2001. It was as straightforward as it was prophetic.

"Rob woke up and said, 'I had the weirdest dream,'" Ellen told me. "I said, 'Tell me about it.'

"He said, 'I was in a building—not the WTC—and a jet ran into it.' He was very disturbed by this dream. We didn't try to analyze the dream. It was bizarre. I just remember thinking how strange it was.

"Something else happened that I can't explain," she continued. "Rob and I were into sailing, and Rob always wanted to have a boat. In August, we were sitting on the lawn of the New York Athletic Club in Pelham, overlooking the Long Island Sound, and I said, 'Let's get a boat. Let's get a day sailer or something,' and Rob said, 'Well, the summer is getting long-in-the-tooth. Let's do it next summer,' and I had this sinking feeling at that moment that there wouldn't be a 'next summer' for us."

Ellen told me that on September 8th, Robert went to his sister Brenda's* house on Long Island for a last swim in her pool before she closed it for the season. Brenda recently had to euthanize her beautiful and loyal golden Labrador, Sadie. Robert had really loved that dog. While Robert was taking his final swim, he stopped suddenly. He looked up at the sky, as Brenda described it, and said, "Sadie, I miss you, but don't worry, I'm going to be with you soon." Brenda, who spoke to me on the phone, said that although she was sitting by the pool, she felt that Robert was in some other place and that his words were not meant for her. Robert's words for Sadie were so odd that Brenda didn't know how to question what he meant.

On September 9th, Rob went to play golf; he and Ellen agreed to meet in the park later. "It was a really beautiful day," she said. "We had these carry chairs that fold up. So I took the Sunday paper and some books and the chairs. We had this spot where we would always sit. When I got there, I couldn't put both chairs down because there was a fellow sitting there . . . so I asked him, 'My husband will be coming soon. Could you kindly move down a bit?' He said, 'Sure.' Rob was always extremely reliable. When he said he would do something or be somewhere, he always did it . . . it never occurred to me to think that he wouldn't be there. But at that moment, it occurred to me, 'What if he doesn't show up? What if he's not here?' It was just this strange moment of intense fear."

For some reason that she can't even begin to explain, when Robert arrived, Ellen found herself talking about the threat of terrorism. "Our world is going to be much more dangerous than our father's," she said. "We are going to be fighting terrorists." She says she has no idea why she was so focused on terrorism.

Deena Burnett, Wife of Tom Burnett

On 9/11, Deena's husband, Tom, one of the heroes of United Airlines Flight 93, was on his way home to Northern California from New York where he had been on business. I've only talked to Deena on the phone, but she was so incredibly lovely and gracious that I wished I could know her better.

"I always worried about my husband dying in a plane crash," Deena told me. "In 1998 right after our third daughter was born, my mother came into the hospital room and said, 'I guess you'll have to have another child so Tom can have a son.' I don't know why I then said what I said, but I told my mother, 'God is not going to give us a son. God knows I can't raise Tom's son by myself.' My mother asked, 'Is something wrong?' I said, 'No, I've just always had a feeling that Tom is going to be killed in a plane crash.' I wasn't thinking about what I said . . . it just came out of me, coming from I don't know where. My mom thought it was some kind of postpartum babble."

In the summer of 2001, both Deena and Tom had some uneasy feelings and began talking about what they would do if either of them died. Tom began to look at ways to increase his life insurance to care for Deena and the children in case something happened to him. He came home one day and asked Deena, "Haven't you noticed that I haven't been coming home for lunch?"

"Yes, of course," Deena told him. "I just thought you were working."

"No," Tom said, "I've been going to Mass."

Then Tom told Deena something that she couldn't quite understand: "I have this feeling," he said, "that God is calling me for something, and I don't know what it is."

"Do you have any idea?" Deena asked him.

"No," Tom replied. "I just think that if I spend more time in church and in prayer, I'll be able to understand what God is telling me."

Tom was a deeply religious and spiritual person, but he rarely, if ever, spoke about his faith. Deena found what Tom was saying scary as well as unusual. "I asked him about it several times," she said. "All he could tell me is that it was going to impact a large number of people and that it had something to do with the White House."

Everybody had always told Tom that he should think about a career in politics. For a moment, Deena wondered if her articulate, smart, and charismatic husband was considering a career change. "No," he told her, "it's nothing like that."

As the summer progressed, Tom became even more anxious. He told Deena that he knew something was going to happen, but he didn't know what it was. On his last night home, which was the Friday before 9/11, Tom was watching a television documentary about how to fly a Boeing jet. "He had seen it several times, but for some reason he was intrigued by it," Deena said.

"Thinking about that last night, I realize that I had this feeling that he wasn't going to come back from this trip. Something kept saying to me, 'This is it.' Then I told myself to put those thoughts out of my mind. He's coming home, I told myself. He always comes home."

Deena isn't sure what her feelings of anxiety represented. Nonetheless, she is certain that God's grace was with both her and her husband. It was as though something was meant to be and she couldn't stop it. "This belief has allowed me not to be angry," she told me.

Tom Burnett

Deena and Tom Burnett at their wedding

Deidre K.*, Wife of Craig K.*

I met Deidre in the fall of 2001 at a meeting of 9/11 families. I immediately liked her, and we stayed in touch. When she heard about this book, she told me she had a story:

"I was madly in love with my husband," Deidre recounted. "I loved him as much as the day I married him. On Labor Day weekend of 2001, Craig and I and our two children, Leslie* and Mark*, were at our beach cottage, swimming and sunning. Swimming was always a family thing. Craig had been an ocean lifeguard, and he wanted the kids to be great swimmers. I was usually the first one out of the water. I would just stand there, looking at the kids and thinking about how great they all looked.

"Late in the afternoon on Sunday, I was standing with towels waiting for them to come out of the water—the three of them. They were walking toward me with the sun shining on them. They were glowing. Everything was glittering and sparkling. I looked at Craig and I thought, 'Oh my God. He's so gorgeous—such a beautiful man, such a wonderful husband and father. What would I do if I lost him?' I remember staring at him as he came toward me. I couldn't understand why I was having these thoughts."

Deidre didn't know until after 9/11 that her husband had felt his own sense of uneasiness; she later learned that as Craig walked on the beach that weekend, he had turned to his son, Mark, and said, "I want you to promise me that if anything happens to me, you'll take care of your mother and your sister."

The following weekend, the children had plans with friends, so Deidre and Craig decided they would go out to the house by themselves. Both children were almost ready for college.

"We were looking forward to being able to spend more time alone," Deidre said. "Soon we would be able to start doing everything we had ever talked about as a couple. We were married young and quickly had children. We were both thinking, 'We're almost there. Our time for us is going to be here soon.' We had the most romantic weekend. We woke up, swam, and played tennis. That Sunday morning, September 9th, the sun was coming through the windows. I remember just getting up, sitting on the bed, and looking out the window.

"Out of nowhere, I had this overwhelming sense of foreboding. I was thinking, 'Oh my God, all of our plans are not going to come true—something terrible is going to happen.' I was convinced. I just knew that what we had talked about was not going to happen. It was physical. It felt so heavy. I said, 'OK, Deidre, get off the bed!' When the building was hit, I flashed back to the premonition. I knew he was not going to make it."

Jennifer Brady, Wife of David Brady

Jennifer Brady lost her forty-one-year-old husband, David, who was a vice president at Merrill Lynch. David worked at the World Financial Center, which was across the street from the World Trade Center. On the morning of 9/11, he left his office at 8:39 A.M. to walk over to the North Tower for a breakfast meeting. Jennifer believes David was on the last elevator that arrived at the restaurant Windows on the World.

David and Jennifer Brady

"My husband never actually said that he expected to die young," Jennifer said. "However, he definitely tried to live his life so there would be absolutely no spiritual regrets. This approach to life intensified during 2001. He began prioritizing the elements in his life. In a sense he was rewriting his priorities—how to be a better person. He began to live as if each day was his last. . . . Toward the end, I felt like he was trying to finish open-ended items, wanting to get his house in order. . . . It was like he was on a mission. . . . I felt that he was finishing parts of his life. For example, David made sure his parents came with us on a vacation that summer (something we had never done before) to the Outer Banks, a place that had meaning to him. It was almost as though he was purposely creating and leaving behind good memories."

David Brady was very clear about his life and how he wanted it lived. He knew, without a doubt, that he wanted to be a good person. He wanted to be a good husband and father; he wanted to be a good son; he wanted to be a good friend. His faith was very important, and he wasn't afraid to let people know what it meant to him.

"You know he never came out and said it, but he became such a perfectionist about his spirituality and wanting to be a better Christian and needing to be accountable for everything in life and his actions," said Jennifer, describing her husband during the last year of his life. "He was very, very religious, and I think he knew he was going to meet his Maker, and he wanted to get his affairs in order in this life."

Janice Green

Janice Green worked for Fiduciary Trust on the ninety-seventh floor of the South Tower off and on for about five years as an on-site application support consultant for a software vendor. She liked her work at Fiduciary, and she loved her coworkers. There was a wonderful sense of camaraderie and fun that she appreciated. She had expected to be there through the end of 2001, but in the fall of 2000, she began to experience debilitating muscle pain. It was initially diagnosed as fibromyalgia. Eventually she learned that she had a form of advanced Lyme disease and babesia. When she worked in downtown Manhattan, Janice owned a condo in Jersey City. Looking out of the windows of her apartment, there was a clear view of the World Trade Center across the river.

To get to work, she had to take a bus as well as the PATH train. Because of her illness, the commute became too difficult. Janice stayed at Fiduciary through May of 2001, training a replacement. Trying to find a new and better lifestyle, she opted to work from home. She bought a house in the Pennsylvania countryside and moved out of her Jersey City condo and into her new house on August 1, 2001.

Janice knew at least forty of the people killed at the WTC; twenty of them were in her department. Many of these victims were good friends as well as coworkers. When describing the dream she had days before 9/11, Janice told me that although she is sensitive to her environment, she does not consider herself psychic. Nonetheless, she had the following dream during the morning hours of Saturday, September 1st.

"In my dream I was back in the condo I had already sold in Jersey City, New Jersey, looking out across the water at Manhattan," Janice remembered. "One wall of my apartment was mostly made up of long windows and French doors, and it faced north. Essentially, my view was of the southern tip of Manhattan, i.e., the World Trade Center and the World Financial Center. As I was looking out the windows, there was a huge explosion. I saw something that looked almost like a mushroom cloud over the city, and I turned to my husband and said, 'Bin Laden just blew up New York. Grab the dogs and get them away from the windows in case they shatter.' I could see something like a cloud or a shock wave making its way toward us across the water. Then I turned, walked a few steps, and bent over, shielded my head with my arms and hands, and waited for some kind of impact."

At that point, Janice woke up, feeling haunted by the dream. It was Saturday, and that afternoon she made herself some lunch and turned on the television. The movie that immediately caught her attention was called *The World Trade Center*. It was about the 1993 attack. At the end of the film, the FBI had taken into custody the last terrorist who was responsible for that attack. They were in a helicopter flying past the Trade Center when the terrorist nodded in the direction of the towers and said, "Next time they'll both come down." When Janice turned off the film, she had a terrible feeling, "like something bad was imminent, and this feeling didn't leave me."

The following Friday, September 7th, Janice's parents came to her house for a visit. While she was in a car with them, running errands, Janice told them about her dream as well as the coincidence of the World Trade Center movie being on television that same day. She also shared with them her horrible sense of impending doom. "I mentioned that I was glad I was out of New York because I had a really bad feeling that wouldn't go away," she said. "Then there was this silence in the car." On Monday evening, September 10th, Janice was hit with what she describes as a "really bad crying spell." She was just incredibly sad and thinks it may somehow be connected to her sense of foreboding. After September 11th, Janice reminded her mother about the conversation in the car and the fact that her parents had not reacted to Janice's description of her dream. She asked her mother if she was quiet because she thought Janice was crazy or because they believed her and were taken aback by it. Janice's mother said it was the latter.

Janice said that, unlike many others, she was aware of Bin Laden before the fall of 2001 from various news stories, so his name wasn't completely unknown to her. I talked to Janice's mother, who clearly remembers hearing Janice describe her dream on the Friday before the World Trade Center attacks. When the first plane went into the North Tower, her television was on, and she was on the phone with Janice. Janice's dream quickly came back into her mind.

Since 9/11, Janice has had other dreams, which have had a profound impact on her. In these dreams, angels have told her that our innate intuition and related messages come from God and the Holy Spirit, which we all have within us.

"We should pay more attention to this and His overwhelming love for us," she told me. "Instead of turning away from Him, which so many have done, we should turn toward Him, pray to Him, and seek his love and guidance."

Janice sent me a photo of a rainbow over the World Trade Center taken from her apartment window, reminding me of the importance of the rainbow in the Bible and God's covenant with man. In her e-mail, she quoted Genesis 9:15–15: "God told Noah and his sons, 'And I will remember my covenant, which is between me and you and every living creature of all flesh and the waters shall no more become a flood to destroy all flesh. And the bow shall be in the cloud; and I will look upon it, that I may remember the everlasting covenant between God and every living creature of all flesh that is upon the earth.'" Janice explained, "It was just so uncanny that the rainbow was right over the Trade Center. It seemed very significant at the time."

Janice Green's view of the WTC from her New Jersey apartment, rainbow overhead

Julia C.

Julia is an editor who has been working with me on this book. One of the reasons why she was attracted to this project concerns a dream that she had. In 2001 Julia was living in Park Slope, Brooklyn. She had recently separated from her husband, and they were thinking about reconciling. She was seeing a therapist to try to figure out the wisdom of this course of action. In the several months that she was in therapy, her therapist kept asking her about her dreams, and she kept telling him that she wasn't having any. Then, on September 9th, she went to bed and had the following dream.

"In the dream I was in the front yard of a country house I had sold a couple of years earlier," Julia began. "I was puttering around the yard, standing next to the long driveway, which was on an incline leading to the house. It was an extraordinarily beautiful day, and I was appreciating the blue sky when suddenly out of nowhere, a huge eighteen-wheel truck came barreling up the driveway; it literally took off and flew into the house, disappearing entirely. The mood of the dream abruptly changed. When I looked at the house, it was now surrounded by tall buildings. Looking at the house, all I could see was this huge, gaping black hole with jagged edges. I couldn't believe that the truck had disappeared in the house. It had been completely swallowed up, and I couldn't see it. Inside the hole, there was a flicker of a fire, and black smoke was beginning to form.

"I had three thoughts," she continued. "(1) I knew I was safe and had not been hurt by the truck; (2) I knew that if anybody had been in the building, they would have been killed, and (3) I couldn't understand how this huge truck had disappeared so that I could no longer see any part of it. I tried to look into the jagged hole, but I could see nothing except that blackness, the small flame, and the smoke that was starting to billow out. I was grateful that neither I nor my husband, nor any of our animals were in the house. This was a very upsetting dream. It woke me up, and I couldn't get the image out of my mind. Because I was seeing my therapist the following day and because I was pleased that I finally had a dream I could remember with some very strong feelings and vivid details, I wrote the dream down.

"On Tuesday, September 11th, I left my house at about 8:00 A.M. to drive to the therapist's office on Manhattan's Upper West Side," she said. "The piece of paper with the dream on it was on the passenger seat. It was a breathtakingly beautiful morning. I had just come out of the Brooklyn Battery Tunnel and was going up West Street about 8:45, and, at 8:46, when I heard and felt the blast as the first plane hit, I had just passed the Marriott Hotel. The North Tower was directly to my right. The explosion was so strong that for an instant it felt as though the car had left the ground. I remember grabbing the wheel and feeling pleased that I hadn't lost control of the car. I had no idea what had happened. Traffic was stopping and people were looking up, but I was too close to the building to look up and see. When I was a little farther north, I stopped the car to see what people were staring at. I could hear sirens, and the first fire trucks were arriving. They looked so small next to the tall buildings. When I looked at the large, gaping black hole in the North Tower, it appeared identical to the image in my dream, and my reactions were remarkably similar. I tried to look into the space to see what was there. I couldn't understand what had been swallowed up into the building. All I could see was a little flicker of flame and smoke. I knew that I was safe; I knew that people were dying in the building. There was nothing I could do except say a prayer."

Lisa Bellan-Boyer

Lisa Bellan-Boyer, a Lutheran parish deacon, who teaches religious studies, was not at the WTC on the morning of September 11th. Nonetheless, she had a strong connection to the site.

Before 9/11, Lisa taught religious studies and served in a storefront congregation in a lower-income neighborhood. She was also very active as a singer of classical music. After 9/11, she served as a chaplain at the medical examiner's office in connection with the World Trade Center response effort. She is currently a lead docent at the Tribute Center at the WTC. Before 9/11, a great deal of her focus was directed toward music; she was a member of the New York Choral Society and, while doing graduate work at NYU, was a member of the NYU Gospel Choir. After 9/11 her priorities changed, and much of her time was spent in volunteer work at the WTC. Working as a chaplain at the WTC was a life-changing experience for Lisa.

"I was so blessed to work with so many people from so many different faith traditions and to have known so many wonderful people—family members and survivors," she said. "To have the privilege of walking in solidarity with them has been extremely profound, and I wouldn't trade the experience of knowing those folks for anything except the dream that this would have never happened."

Lisa is very familiar with the area around the World Trade Center because she has spent so much time commuting from New York to New Jersey, using the PATH train station that existed under the WTC. Lisa had two separate premonitions concerning the WTC. The first took place more than eight years before 9/11. It was on the evening of February 25, 1993, a day before the first bombing of the WTC. On that evening, the NYU Gospel Choir had been invited to sing at the Hard Rock Cafe. It was a great concert. Lisa did a solo, and she remembered being in a terrific mood: "When we were finished singing, the Hard Rock management sat us down at a big round table and said to the starving college students 'order anything you want—it's all on the house.' So we went crazy. It was really cool to sit there and eat with Elvis's suit and John Lennon's guitar and all those things. Anyway, we had a lovely time that night."

Afterward, Lisa got on the subway down to the World Trade Center so she could get on a PATH train to New Jersey, where she was living with her husband. It was after midnight; she had just missed a train and had to wait. She sat down on a bench on the platform and was happily reminiscing about the evening when she was overcome by a troubling vision: "I guess psychologists would call it an ideation, but a very intense and overwhelming thought came into my head, unlike anything I'd ever thought before, and I couldn't believe I was thinking what I was thinking, but my thought was, Gee, there's like 110 stories of building over my head and what if it all came crashing down someday?"

While she was thinking this, Lisa said she had a visual image of debris and beams and broken cables in a giant crater, not unlike the debris pothole that would eventually exist at the WTC. As she thought about the humans who lived and worked around her, she was shocked that she was having such thoughts. "I couldn't believe that I had this thought. I asked myself, 'What's up with you? Are you out of your mind? How could you even think such a thing?'" When the PATH train pulled into the station, Lisa leaped into it, eager to get away, still berating herself for having a mind that was able to conjure up such a hideous image. Some twelve hours later, the first World Trade Center bombing took place. One of the areas most heavily hit was the PATH station in which Lisa had been waiting.

I asked Lisa if she had ever had similar kinds of thoughts. "I did have one other experience," she told me. "I think it was during the mid-1980s. I was in NYC on my way home to New Jersey from an art class—when I had that same kind of very strong ideation. The thought came into my head, 'Here in New York, people have guns. It would be very easy to get shot in some crossfire, you know, if guns started to go off when you're out on the street,' and I shuddered. I was right near the Ninth Street PATH station, and I dashed down the stairs." When Lisa got home, she turned on the TV to watch the eleven o'clock news and saw the breaking report about a shooting that had occurred exactly where she had been standing minutes after she had gone into the PATH station.

Right before Labor Day 2001, Lisa and her husband, Paul, who was a divinity student at the time, took a short vacation on the Jersey shore. While they were there, Lisa, who is not a strong swimmer, got caught in a riptide and almost drowned. As Lisa describes it, she had a near-death experience. "I went under the water. I saw the light and was pulled toward it. While I found it terrifying, the light was also drawing me, and I was relaxing into that. Fortunately, there was an alert lifeguard, and my husband was about twenty feet behind me. They pulled me out."

Lisa and her husband returned from their vacation on the Sunday of Labor Day weekend. Since they had the rental car until Monday, they decided to take a trip to Staten Island. When they returned to Manhattan on the ferry, it was sunset. Lisa and her husband stood at the bow, holding hands. Anyone who has ever taken the Staten Island Ferry back to Manhattan at sunset remembers the colors of the setting sun reflecting off the Twin Towers. A couple of nights later, after Lisa fell asleep, she had the following dream.

"What I saw in the dream were two predatory birds," she recalled. "They weren't noble-looking like eagles or large owls. They were more pterodactyl-like, and I remember shuddering in the dream when I saw them. They were very sordid, scabby, and vultury. They were just the ugliest birds I've ever imagined, looking like a cross between a vulture and pterodactyl. One of them stretched out its scabby-looking wings and made as though they were the hands on a clock. It started to move one of its wings as though it was the ticking second hand on a clock. The other bird was looking at me and squawking a horrible kind of squawk. The feeling or message I got was that 'time is running out.' And that's really all there was to the dream, just the two huge and frightening predatory birds and the message that time is running out. I woke up and thought, 'Wow, that's a really odd dream.'"

It wasn't until later that Lisa came to see the birds as lethal aircraft.

Allison Wallice, Wife of John Wallice

(Left to right) Christian, John, and Jack Wallice

Allison's husband, John Wallice, was an international equities trader at Cantor Fitzgerald. He worked on the 104th floor of the North Tower. He and his wife had three sons: Christian, Jack, and Patrick. Allison talked to me about her memories.

"September 10, 2001, was a crazy, busy, hectic day," she said. "I had appointments all day with the boys. We did the dentist and the doctor, and the boys had sports practice. I didn't get home until six, and John was home before me. He went to work very early each day because he did those London hours."

"The night of September 10th was unusual. Even though it was a weeknight and I had been running around all day, I decided to make a special dinner. We put the children to bed early and then we sat down with candlelight and wine and grilled lamb chops. I would normally never do this kind of thing on a weeknight, but for some reason, I made an extra effort. It was a special night, and we talked for hours about the possibility of adopting another child, something I had wanted to do. I will never forget that night or the details or the strangeness—a candlelight dinner on a Monday when I was totally stressed. It was very symbolic."

Before they fell asleep, John turned to her.

"I'll never forget it," she said. "He cupped—held my face in his hands and he said, 'I—love—you. Do—you—know—how—much—I—love—you?' He enunciated each word. I remember being so overwhelmed by how he said it that I felt like I couldn't even say 'me too' so I looked at him and said, 'I know. I know.' Neither one of us was able to fall asleep. I kept thinking I can't fall asleep. Then at about 4:00 A.M., I could hear his breathing had changed, and I thought, 'Oh this poor guy. He just fell asleep, and I know he's got to get up in half an hour.' I started to drift into a really relaxed state where my mind was kind of floating in this dark place, and I felt very light. I wasn't dreaming, and I know I wasn't dreaming, but I also wasn't totally awake. I was just kind of floating in this quasilike dream. As I floated, I saw a light and I said to myself, 'Let's go toward that light.' Then in my head, I'm thinking, 'What are you doing? This is a dying person's dream! You're not dying!!' And with that I woke up and the alarm went off. When I told John, he said, 'Yeah, that's a weird dream.'"

John and Allison spoke several times that morning as they regularly did every day, but she could not get the dream out of her head. "John used to call us around seven," she said. "We'd talk at home.

Allison and John Wallice

Then we'd have breakfast and call him again. Then we'd call him from the car. After the boys went to school, I called him and said, 'That was the weirdest dream.' We didn't speak again."

PREMONITIONS LEFT BEHIND

After my husband passed on, I kept finding pieces of his writing scattered about the house. Not only did I find completed poems, I found dozens of scraps of paper in unlikely places with short poems, beginnings of poems, and notes. Several of the people who agreed to share their memories and experiences with me also told me about discovering writings or art that their loved ones left behind.

Charles Wolf, Husband of Katherine Wolf

Charles lost his beloved wife, Katherine, who was working at Marsh & McLennan on the ninty-seventh floor of the North Tower. Katherine and Charles met in New York on July 27, 1988. Katherine, an extremely gifted pianist who lived in London, was visiting here with a London operetta group that she worked for as an accompanist. They were staging a joint production with the Village Light Opera Group, of which Charles was a member.

Charles and Katherine Wolf

The minute Charles saw Katherine, he knew he wanted to get to know her; within a few moments of talking to her, he could barely think of anything else. Their courtship took place in London and New York, and eventually Katherine decided to move here. They were legally married in September of 1989 in Wales and followed that up with a large Blessing of the Marriage Ceremony in October 1990 at the Cathedral of St. John the Divine. Charles sang to her "The Desert Song."

Early on, when the couple was talking about their future, Charles said he would like an apartment that looked out over Manhattan with the river in the background. Katherine replied that she didn't like the idea of being on a high floor and often talked about her fear of being trapped by fire. Despite her fears, on August 9, 2001, Katherine accepted a job that would put her up on a very high floor. Her official start day was Monday, August 20th. She had a week's training in a building located on the Avenue of the Americas and then, on September 1st, started her job in the Towers. Her hours were set at nine to five. At the end of the first week, her boss asked her if she could change her hours and start at eight-thirty, and she agreed.

Katherine kept a dream journal in which she jotted down dreams that she remembered. The last entry was made on August 10th, the day after she accepted a job at the World Trade Center. Here is Katherine's dream from that date.

I held a long tubular atom bomb with a pointed end and then I released it. I told the people I needed to tell that I had released the bomb. Another bomb was on its way to our house. I could see its lights on the radar screen. It could track by smell. I remembered how to trick it. The bomb did not go off but it hit where I had just been sitting. I could see the bomb in the shape of a paper plane with a sort of brake at the end to stop it from going off.

On the morning of September 11th, Katherine was not in a good mood. Charles remembers that she wanted to turn on the television, saying, " 'My mind is very uneasy. I need the television noise to settle my mind.' She was frazzled . . . she was not a happy camper that morning," Charles told me. Before she left, as he gave her a hug, Charles noticed that she was leaving a little earlier than normal.

"She got there around 8:25 or 8:30. She was never late. She was British. It was almost as if she was supposed to be there. Everything just put her there."

Friday, August 10

I held a large tubular atom bomb with a pointed end, and then I released it. I told the people I needed to tell that I had released the bomb. Another bomb was on its way to our house — I could see its lights on the radar screen. It could track by smell. I remembered how to trick it. The bomb did not go off, but it hit where I had just been sitting.

I could see the bomb is the shape of a paper plane with a sort of brake as the end to stop it from going off.

The entry from Katherine's dream journal

Josephine*, Stepmother of BettyAnne*

Josephine is the stepmother of BettyAnne, thirty-two, who worked for Cantor Fitzgerald. I didn't know BettyAnne, but like my husband she worked on the 105th floor of the North Tower.

Josephine truly loved BettyAnne, who is remembered for her sweet, enthusiastic, and generous spirit. She loved to write and she loved to sing. After BettyAnne passed on, her family went through her apartment and found some inexplicable items. Just as it did in Katherine's dream, a paper airplane takes on an ominous significance. Josephine showed me the memorabilia box where BettyAnne had kept a few items from work, mostly representative of major events: photos of people at a company Christmas event (none of whom I recognized), photos of people at a wedding, several thank-you notes from people for gifts BettyAnne had given them, some trinkets, and a piece of legal paper folded like a paper airplane. Seeing it was a reminder of my visits to the 105th floor to see Eamon and his friends. They hardly ever left their seats, eating lunch at their desks, always anticipating the next phone call from a client, hollering out transaction details to administrative staff while engaging in endless antics to deflect the boredom. Sharing crazy handwritten cartoons, throwing spitballs, and sailing paper airplanes around the room were all common diversions used to break up the monotony of the workday.

BettyAnne's family had been taken aback by the paper airplane she kept. Unfolded, on the inside, there was a note from a girlfriend in the office wishing BettyAnne a good trip to Texas. In its paper airplane form, the paper is stunning. American Airlines is written on the side in capital letters. Along the top of the airplane are windows. The first framed a cartoon of a pilot—looking as if a bag had been placed over his face. Behind him, someone is pointing a gun at his head. In the next window was a cartoon of BettyAnne enjoying a drink, oblivious to what is going on in the cockpit. This was followed by a third window where an alien creature is sitting. In the fourth seat is a profile of a man with MATT DILLON written over his head, obviously symbolic of the Texas trip. Finally, the last drawing is of a bird with its wings spread out. Written next to it are the words DEAD BIRD.

Both Josephine and I agreed that this "airplane" was strange. Why

The paper airplane from BettyAnne's memorabilia box

was there a drawing of a man pressing a gun into the head of a pilot? Why did BettyAnne keep it? Was it reflective of some kind of premonition?

Josephine had something else she wanted me to see from the memorabilia box. It was a piece of paper that reads:

> You can have whatever you
> want Ground zero leaves
> every day is your birthday
> and you were just born

I read this aloud, and Josephine and I just looked at each other.

"What does this mean?" I asked.

"I don't know," Josephine replied.

We have no way of knowing why BettyAnne kept the drawing of the American Airlines plane or what she intended by her scribbled words about Ground Zero, written long before the term became associated with the World Trade Center.

Marilyn Bullis, Mother of Dianne Bullis Snyder

Dianne Bullis Snyder

Dianne Bullis Snyder was working as a flight attendant on American Airlines Flight 11, which crashed into the North Tower of the WTC.

Marilyn remembers her daughter as a happily married mother of two young children, who was usually very upbeat about life. However, during the summer of 2001, her normally positive daughter seemed different. In August of 2001, Marilyn remembers Dianne asking her to visit her family at the Massachusetts beach community where they lived.

"She was very quiet—not her usual happy self," Marilyn said.

Marilyn showed me something Dianne wrote in July of 2001.

*Live life to the fullest; no one knows
what will happen tomorrow.
Accept what comes; use it to master
the art of living.
Worrying won't help.*

Live one day at a time.
Share hope with people.
Remember there's a light at the
end of the tunnel.
No one knows the power of the
individual.
Keep trying.
It's all right to show emotions.
Don't stop dreaming.
God is always there to help.
Don't wait for tragedy; say
it today. "I love you and I'm glad you're alive."

When Dianne wrote this, she placed it on the refrigerator, but it slipped off and fell between the refrigerator and the counter, where Dianne's husband, John, found it months later.

"Dianne was such a wonderful person," Marilyn said. "Her family and friends all felt this way about her."

"It's as if she knew something was going to happen," I said. And I thought about the last line of her poem. *Don't wait for tragedy; say it today. I love you and I'm glad you're alive.*

After Dianne's death, Marilyn received a letter from an old college friend of Dianne's. "He was so devastated by Dianne's death," Marilyn said. "He eventually came to visit me in 2006. 'I have a memento from Dianne to give you,' he said to me. And he handed me a painting she had done in high school. It was a landscape of a red barn on green grass surrounded by a fence. Above were cotton ball clouds dotting a bright blue sky. It looked exactly like the barn Dianne's husband was building. . . . I gave the painting to John. I viewed it as a sign from Dianne that she wanted him to get on with his life."

Live life to the fullest; no one knows
what will happen tomorrow.
Accept what comes; use it to master
the art of living.
Worrying won't help.
Live one day at a time.
Share hope with people.
Remember there's a light at the
end of the tunnel
No one knows the power of the
individual
Keep trying.
Its all right to show emotions
Don't stop dreaming
God is always there to help.
Don't wait for tragedy say
it today "I love you and I'm
glad your alive Buffie Snyder
Written by Dianne July 2

Dianne's handwritten note from July 2001

PREMONITIONS HEEDED

Not all premonitions are ignored, even when they are not correctly identified. Eamon was not the first person in his family with premonitions. One of Eamon's favorite stories involved the Irish grandmother he adored, Annie Morgan Litchfield. Everyone said that Annie had a strong Celtic sixth sense. When Annie was in her early twenties and working in Dublin, she met a young man who was destined to become Eamon's grandfather. His name was Peter McEneaney, and he came from Castle Blayney in County Monaghan. Like many other young people in Ireland at that time, Peter and Annie separately decided that they would make the long trip across the Atlantic Ocean to New York City in order to make their

*home in America. The plan was that Peter would go first; Annie would
follow. Annie and Peter were not yet engaged. In fact, they didn't really
know each other very well, and yet there must have been some kind of
connection, because Annie expected Peter to be waiting for her when she
arrived.*

*But when the time came for Annie to leave, she was overwhelmed
by a strange sensation. She couldn't really describe it. All she knew was
that she felt compelled to change her plans at the very last minute and,
instead, go visit her mother, even though they had already said good-
bye only a few days before. Something told her not to get on this particular ship. The year was 1912, and the ship, of course, was the* Titanic.
Annie had followed her instincts.

Barret Naylor

*Recently I was at a dinner lecture and was seated near Barret Naylor, a
man I had never met. We started to talk, and when he heard my name, he
told me that he had known my husband. They took the same commuter
train to New York. "We saw each other from time to time," he said. He
went on to tell me how much he liked Eamon and how sorry he was about
what had happened. He asked how I was doing and what I was doing,
and I began to tell him about this book project.*

"I have something to tell you," he said.

He proceeded to share his story, which his wife, Kim, who was also
at the dinner, corroborated. For many years, he had been employed by
a midsize financial company down in the complex of buildings next
to the World Trade Center. Like Eamon, in order to get to work, he
took the commuter train to Grand Central Station in New York and
then transferred to a subway to get downtown. On the day of the '93
bombing at the World Trade Center, when he got to Grand Central
Station, he was suddenly overcome by a generalized sense of malaise.
He couldn't really put his finger on what he was feeling, but he knew

he wasn't feeling well enough to go to work, so he returned home.

He didn't think much about what he had experienced. Nor did he actively connect it to the '93 bombing. He hadn't felt well; he had luckily returned home; end of story. But when the morning of 9/11 arrived, he had the same sort of feelings and took the same course of action. Once again, he got on the commuter train; once again, when he arrived at Grand Central, he was overcome by a general sense of malaise; once again, instead of getting on the subway, he turned around and went home. When he walked through the door of his house, he found his worried wife watching the television. The South Tower had just collapsed.

Both he and his wife assured me that at no other time had he turned around and not gone to work. Interestingly, he doesn't have a history of having any foreknowledge of future events. He's a practical down-to-earth person. Nonetheless, he can't deny his direct experience.

All of these individuals had premonitions—a shared sense of foreboding, defying the odds of chance. As the well-known psychiatrist Carl Jung explained, using the term synchronicity, *"The concept of synchronicity indicates a meaningful coincidence of two or more events, where something other than probability of chance is involved."*

The premonitions, clairvoyance, and precognition demonstrated by so many prior to 9/11 seem to imply an underlying spiritual connection.

CHAPTER SEVEN

Signs of Spiritual Connection

It's human nature to look for signs of life after death. When someone you love has passed on, it seems inconceivable that the soul-to-soul connection the two of you shared is gone. At moments such as these it's not unusual to look up into the heavens, where you believe your loved one has surely gone, and plead, "Give me a sign."

Men and women who have received what they believe are credible "signs" are usually quick to acknowledge that they can understand why others might question, if not their experience, then their interpretation of what it means. Couldn't it all just be coincidence? But when you are on the receiving end of something that appears totally inexplicable, coincidence seems almost more far-fetched than the possibility of a "sign" from a larger reality to which we are all inextricably linked.

In the days, weeks, and months immediately following 9/11, as my friends and I were trying to make sense of the tragedy, many of us were admittedly looking for "signs" of a divine presence that would give us comfort and direction. And we kept finding evidence of these signs. I gasped when I viewed the large cross that a rescue worker found at the site. Naturally formed by shards of steel beams that came from the remains of the North Tower, it was standing upright in the rubble. That's how it fell. When people saw it, it seemed like a miracle as well as a sign that God was somehow present. A Catholic priest, Father Brian Jordan, blessed the cross; rescue workers and grieving visitors stood before it to pray.

The cross found in the pile at Ground Zero

During this same time period I read a story in the New York Times about a sixteen-year-old boy standing in a church delivering a eulogy at a memorial service for his mother who died in the WTC. There, before hundreds of mourners, something very special happened. As soon as he said the word *mother*, a tiny sparrow flew toward him and landed on his head. He was able to catch the bird in his hands and set it free. Later, the New York Times quoted him as saying, "I'm not a religious person. I don't believe in things like that. But there is no other explanation than that my mother was with me."

I was haunted by the idea of the bird landing on this young man's head. Most of us would be hard-pressed to find another example of bird behavior that resembles what took place at this memorial service for a beloved mother. Yet, in myth and history, birds are often seen as symbols of the divine or messengers with the ability to connect to a Higher Power.

Lisa Bellan-Boyer told me about being with her husband, Paul, both chaplains, at a ceremony on a sunny day in May of 2002 honoring the dead and closing the site at the World Trade Center. "At the end of the ceremony, they released eleven doves," she said. "If I were a dove who had been cooped up in a cage, I would probably take off in a minute, but these doves stayed together. The doves flew high in a spiral pattern over the footprint of the North Tower. Then they swooped down over where the plaza had been and then flew over to the footprint of the South Tower and spiraled again. They went over to the plaza again and then they just flew up. We watched and watched. At some point they were so high, they looked as though they just disappeared into the ether."

Birds are not the only winged creatures associated with profoundly spiritual moments or after-death communication. One morning in the fall of 2001, I received a phone call from my friend Don Lee, telling me about the butterflies flying over the rubble of the WTC. Don lives in downtown Manhattan, and both he and his wife, Kathie, who had been rollerblading near the Hudson River, had seen them. Don sounded very excited. "You won't believe all the butterflies flying around here," he said. "They are all over the place from Ground Zero down to the river. Hasn't anybody else told you about them?" Later, both he and Kathie confirmed what they saw. "It was unbelievable," Don said. "There were hundreds, maybe thousands of butterflies. They filled the sky. They were the most beautiful colors," Kathie said. "You know what we thought?" she whispered. "That they were the people; they were the souls, and they were trying to help us cope with the pain and anguish we felt for them by appearing as beautiful, floating, free creatures of the world still here with us."

Others also told me about all the delicate winged creatures that suddenly appeared, with no understandable explanation, and spent a day dancing around the piles of smoking debris. Workers on their hands and knees sifting and raking through the piles stopped what they were doing to stare. To many of the workers, the butterflies looked almost as if they were emerging from the site. What were they doing in the smoke? Why would butterflies choose to be at Ground Zero? Nobody had any answers. I was told that many of the workers also immediately began referring to them as "the souls." When I did a little bit of research, I discovered that butterflies hold a special place in the spiritual beliefs of many cultures. In Ireland they are, indeed, thought of as souls.

Elaine Mills, an artist living in Connecticut, told me about the unique relationship she developed with a butterfly in the summer of 2001. She was sitting in her yard one day with her dog, her cat, and her parrot when suddenly this beautiful butterfly appeared and landed on her head. She was surprised, but then the butterfly flew to her hand, where it stayed. Eventually, the butterfly flew away, but it returned the following day. For three months, the butterfly showed up at her door every evening at six-thirty. It was amazing. One day, she was cooking dinner when she saw the butterfly at the door. She remembers joking to her husband, "I have to go and tell the butterfly to wait." She took a photo of the butterfly and went to the library to look it up. It was called a Red Admiral. After three months, the butterfly disappeared and didn't return until two weeks later. When it reappeared, its wings were tattered and torn. Elaine believes that the butterfly returned to say good-bye. She showed me a video of the butterfly peacefully sitting on her hand. The last time Elaine saw the butterfly was right before September 11th, and she connects it to the event.

Rainbows, like butterflies, are frequently seen surrounding a loved one's death. People interested in Buddhism and Tibet have probably read about the great lamas and Buddhist teachers who were said to have incredible powers, including being able to create rainbows at the time of their death. In 2008, many of us watched the televised memorial service for much admired author and NBC newsman Tim Russert. At the end of the service, mourners heard a moving ukulele version of "Somewhere Over the Rainbow." Outside, they were greeted by a huge double rainbow, arching over Washington, DC. How could this not be interpreted as a spiritual moment?

The last photo I received of my husband was sent to me by Diane Wall; her husband, Glen Wall, was another of Eamon's closest friends at Cantor Fitzgerald. Diane called me ahead of time, telling me that I had to see this picture. It was from the last golfing trip to Ireland that Glen, Eamon, Farrell Lynch, Timmy O'Brien, Eamon's brother Patrick, and several other friends took in 2000. When I pulled the photograph out of the envelope I couldn't believe it. Eamon was standing in his favorite place, Ireland, and the rainbow seemed to be coming from his soul.

I also feel connected to Eamon through music. He loved Van Morrison. When I hear Van sing, sometimes I immediately get a sense of Eamon's presence. Sometimes it's so strong that I expect to hear my husband's voice singing along. I remember one day while I was driving into New York City with my daughter, Jennifer. She began to share her sadness that she didn't have her dad with her to see her grow and to share the important moments in her life. I told her that her dad was always with her. When we turned on the radio, to our joint amazement, that familiar raspy voice burst through the stillness in the car, singing, "You get me on your wavelength . . ." I'll never forget the smile on Jenny's face as we looked at each other.

Eamon's Irish rainbow

FINDING THE EXTRAORDINARY IN THE ORDINARY

The butterfly "friend" on Elaine Mills's hand

What is it that makes someone identify a small daily event as a sign? Under most circumstances, when you see a group of robins foraging on your lawn or a butterfly landing on a bush, you don't think, "Oh my! There must be a divine connection!" So why do some events appear to be extraordinary "signs" of spiritual significance while others just seem ordinary and not worth noticing? People who feel they have been on the receiving end of signs typically say that these things occur at particularly auspicious moments. Many, for example, say that the "sign" appears in response to an expressed request or a palpable need. They say that there is something worth noting about how and where the "sign" shows up. Even the most mundane "sign" has an unusual or inexplicable quality attached to it. The primary quality that people associate with "signs" is that the sign itself typically also has some meaning to you, the person who has passed on, or the shared relationship.

Some of the most common types of signs that people receive include: scents, sound, electrical manipulations, computers, coins, butterflies, birds, animals, insects, rainbows, phones, photos, and numbers. Here are a few of the stories from people who have shared their experiences with me.

Paula Scott, Mother of Ruth McCourt, Grandmother of Juliana McCourt

Paula Scott and granddaughter, Juliana McCourt

Some signs are so unique that they give even the most skeptical pause. Paula Scott received such a sign soon after the death of her daughter, Ruth McCourt, and her four-year-old granddaughter, Juliana, on United Airlines Flight 175.

Paula lives in a light-filled house; you can't help but notice the beautiful houseplants and the windows with the view of her well-tended and lovely garden, complete with rosebushes, feeders, and a very popular birdbath. She is also a terrific cook, and the two times I visited with her, she insisted on preparing lunch. Born and raised in Ireland, Paula Scott is a deeply religious woman who receives tremendous strength from her relationship with God. "He's always there to watch over us," she said.

Juliana had an unusually close relationship with her beautiful and elegant grandmother. When the little girl was two, Paula came from Colorado to Connecticut to be Juliana's "Granny Nanny." Every weekday morning, Paula arrived at the McCourt household at seven-thirty to give Juliana breakfast, and she was there until her parents returned home at the end of the day. When they were together, Juliana and her grandmother sometimes spoke about a fanciful creature known as the "Thread Faery." "I don't remember when I first heard about the Thread Faery, but she has always been part of my life," Paula told me. "Juliana and I read about faeries, and we shared a little world of make-believe. The Thread Faery was part of this. Whenever we found threads— some of them tiny delicate pink threads that came off her little faery dresses—we would hold them up, and say, 'Look what the Thread Faery left. She must have been dancing around at night, shedding these small threads.' I would take these little 'magical' threads and put them in my Bible or in the little daybook I kept for Juliana, in which we drew or wrote down interesting things that happened each day."

Paula had a reverence for these "special threads," holding each one precious to her heart.

Paula said that after the death of her daughter and granddaughter, she was so overcome with grief that she couldn't really be alone. One of her best friends, Alice, offered to stay with her for as long as she needed. A day or two after 9/11, Paula remembers waking up in the morning and going into the bathroom. "I was absolutely in bits," she said. "There was a knock on the door and Alice told me to come quickly. While making the bed, Alice looked down and saw several pieces of golden thread. There was no gold fabric in the room . . . the Thread Faery had visited. When I saw these threads, I immediately knew that my little girl must have become an angel. In those days, I could hardly see or talk. I knew I had to work really hard to be as good as I could be. Harder! I would say I had an angel on each shoulder, and I really needed them."

After talking to Paula, I spoke to Alice to confirm what happened. "I knew about Paula, Juliana, and the Thread Faery," Alice said. "When I saw the thread, I had to tell Paula. From the expression on her face when she saw the golden thread, I knew that it had deep meaning for her."

Since that day, threads continue to appear to Paula to remind her that indeed the Faery Angel is watching over her. "It is a fantastic comfort to me to know that I have my own special Angel," she said. "I have great faith that Ruth and Juliana are in a very good place. They've been handed back to God and I don't begrudge Him. When you give something to somebody, you give it with graciousness."

Paula also had an incident with a butterfly that she views as a sign from her granddaughter. At Juliana's memorial service, Paula was being interviewed by a reporter who was overcome with emotion. As the woman sobbed, a yellow butterfly appeared and circled her head; then it circled Paula's head. Then it repeated the process. The cameraman was so taken aback that he asked if he should use his camera to follow the butterfly.

The memorial service was also attended by several of Juliana's teachers. One of them told Paula about another butterfly that came and visited Juliana's classroom three days after the little girl died. The teacher said that as she walked through the garden to her class a yellow butterfly landed on her shoulder. She felt immediately that this had something to do with Juliana. The butterfly stayed on her shoulder until she entered the classroom. Then it flew over the children and dipped down to each one, as if it was saying, "Hello, I'm here. Don't worry." She watched it flying up and down, up and down over the children's heads. The butterfly remained in class until the end of the school day. After the last child left the classroom, it finally flew away.

Marjorie Farley, Mother of Paige Farley Hackel

Paige Farley Hackel, a spiritual counselor, was Ruth McCourt's best friend and Juliana's godmother. Paige, Ruth, and Juliana were going to California together, but they couldn't all get seats on the same plane. Paige was flying alone on American Airlines Flight 11.

Marjorie Farley and Paige Farley Hackel
on Marjorie's birthday

"Paige did a lot of volunteer work and one of her organizations was called Victory Programs," Marjorie told me. "It's an organization that helps people with huge problems and great need. About two years after 9/11, they were doing a benefit, and a part of the benefit was for the fund they were setting up. It was called Paige's Fund. One day I went out to the mailbox, and there was an envelope from Victory Programs containing an invitation to this event. The theme for this event was butterflies. As I opened the invitation, I swear to God this happened, a little yellow butterfly flew over and landed on the pocket of my blouse. I started talking to the butterfly. It stayed on my pocket as I walked along. When I went back into the house, it flew away. I still say, 'Hi, Paige,' every time I see a yellow butterfly.

"Two days before 9/11 my children gave me a party to celebrate my seventieth birthday. Paige thought of Céline Dion's 'Because You Loved Me' as 'our' song. At the party, Paige, who had never done anything like this before, had set it up to lip-synch the song. She called me up and 'sang' the song to me. Afterward, she invited all the mothers and daughters to dance together to the song. It was a wonderful moment. When I got in my car (a birthday present from my children) to leave, Paige came over to say good-bye. I turned on the ignition, and at that moment, Céline Dion, almost on cue, came on the radio, singing once again, 'Because You Loved Me.' So Paige and I sang it back and forth to each other. I closed the door and I said, 'I love you,' and she said, 'I love you; have a safe trip.' And I drove out of the driveway, sort of like a movie. That was our last time together. Every time I hear that song, it feels like a sign from Paige."

Marni M.*, Stepdaughter of Louise D.*

Not that long ago, I received an e-mail from Marni, whose stepmother, Louise, died on American Airlines Flight 11. I had asked Marni whether she ever has an awareness of Louise's presence. Marni wrote back to tell me that after Louise's death, she had stayed with her father for about ten days in his house because she worried about his being alone. On a beautiful September day when Marni finally returned to her own home, she decided to go for a run and relax. When the run was finished, she "cooled down" by walking the block or two toward her own home. She was still worried about her dad. Her e-mail said:

> Thoughts crept into my mind on whether it was truly OK for my dad to be alone. . . . I just kept thinking about his dinnertime . . . alone. I was not paying attention to anything going on around me . . . just focusing in on that thought. As I was about to step into my driveway, I tripped and fell on my palms at the lip of my driveway. My eyes looked down, and there, resting on the tar, was a penny. Now I have to tell you I NEVER pick up change that I see

on the ground because I feel someone else that really needs it will find it. I never believed in the "Good Luck" thing! But something made me pick up this VERY thin and worn coin. It was obviously old. I needed for some reason to study this and squinted to read the year imprinted. A gasp escaped my throat as I realized that the year was 1955, the year that Louise was born. I started to cry because I knew right then that she had sensed my worry about my father and wanted me to know that she was "watching" over him.

I know that you do not know me ... But I have to tell you that until that personal experience, I just wouldn't have believed anyone telling me that story. I would have passed it off as "coincidental."

Marni said she called experts in Boston to ask just how rare it would be to find a coin from 1955. They told her that although some were still in circulation, most were owned by various collectors throughout the country. Like Marni, I checked the availability of the 1955 penny and was told that it is quite unusual to find one. It is known as a "wheatie" because of the circle of wheat on the back, and no wheaties were minted after 1958. Additionally, an error was made on some of the 1955 pennies, which created some especially rare coins. Because these flawed coins can be worth thousands of dollars, collectors have managed to gather most of the 1955 pennies, searching for the more valuable ones.

For Marni, the 1955 penny had a more important spiritual value. It appeared at the moment when she was most intensely focused on her stepmother's death as well as on her father's well-being. When it appeared, it seemed to speak directly to her concerns. It made her feel that Louise was still caring for those she loved. "I worried at first about Louise, always knowing that she lived life to the fullest, but hoping she 'crossed over' or whatever you want to call it," Marni said. "From that day forward, I knew she was in heaven."

Gayle Barker, Sister of William Anthony Karnes (Tony)

So many people have told me about
flickering lights when there is abso-
lutely no problem with the electricity.
Several of the psychics and mediums
who have talked to me have said that
the spirit world operates on a differ-
ent frequency and that static and other
electrical manipulations are common
forms of after-death communication.
Gayle remembers a moment at the
memorial service for her brother Wil-

Tony Karnes

liam Anthony Karnes, a native of Tennessee, who was a software trainer
for Marsh & McLennan. Everybody called him Tony.

"In the memorial service we had here in Knoxville, Tony's partner, John, was giving a eulogy, and toward the end of it, the lights in the church . . . just kind of blinked out. They just went out for a second and then came back on," Gayle remembered. This seemed strange to Gayle. It seemed even stranger when John told her something that immediately came into his mind. Tony liked to play a trick on him. Sometimes when John was a taking a shower Tony thought it was funny to reach into the bathroom and turn off the light switch, leaving John sputtering in the dark.

Alessandra Benedetti, Wife of Paul Benedetti

After her husband Paul died on September 11th, Alessandra became more
aware of blinking lights. The lights would flash or they would just go on
and off very quickly. The same thing would happen with the television
or a floor lamp.

"At first I thought it was some kind of electrical glitch, but then I couldn't help but notice that it mostly happened when I was thinking a lot about Paul," Alessandra said. "One day I was in the house by myself; it was late afternoon, early evening, and I was watching a television program that focused on a member of a punk rock group that Paul really liked. I thought, "Oh Paul, you would really love to see this." I felt so bad that he wasn't there to watch it with me that I said it out loud. Two seconds after that, the television went black. I thought for sure something was wrong with it or the cable box, but it was a new cable box. Then, just as suddenly as the television went black, it went back on. The segment of the show about the musician was finished, but the new segment was about 9/11. That's when I realized that all the glitches with the lights and the television was Paul. He was trying to get my attention, and I hadn't been paying attention."

Rose DeFazio, Mother of Jason DeFazio

Rose's son, Jason, was a bond trader at Cantor Fitzgerald who had worked his way up from the mailroom. He was twenty-nine; he and his wife, Michele, had been married for three months. Jay, as everyone called him, was a joyous, life-affirming person who was devoted to his family. Both Rose and Michele have had numerous experiences with electricity.

Rose DeFazio and her son, Jason

Rose sometimes asks her son to be with her, and she often feels rewarded by signs that indicate his presence. "One day when I was very, very sad and depressed about Jay's death, I was talking to him, like I often do, telling him how much I missed him," Rose began. "When I walked out of the bathroom located off the master bedroom, I turned off the little Blessed Mother night-light I keep there. It went on again. I turned it off again. It came on again. I called my husband to show him. He turned it off, and the same thing happened. I think that it was my son's way of telling me to be strong and that I am on this earth for a reason."

Rose has a collection of angels that she keeps on a shelf. One of them, a green stained-glass angel, seems to have a life of its own. The angel, which is about five inches tall with a heavy metal base, doesn't want to stay on the shelf where it belongs. More times than Rose can count, she has found it as much as ten feet away, across the room by the sliding glass doors. Rose is sure that her son is somehow involved in this; her feeling was confirmed by a psychic who told Rose that her son Jay's spirit could often be found near the sliding door. When they find the green angel on the floor, Rose's grandchildren and other family members refer to its wandering ways, saying, "The angel flew today."

Rose shared a favorite green angel story: "Jay and my brother, Anthony, had a special relationship, and Jay would always tease his uncle about one thing or another. One day when Anthony was visiting, he was out on the deck and got a splinter in his foot. Anthony came inside, sat down on a love seat, and started complaining about his splinter. We all started making fun of Anthony's complaining. Out of the blue, with no plausible explanation, the green

Rose's green angel

angel flew across the room, hit Anthony's leg, and landed by his foot. How could that happen?"

To family members who were familiar with Jason's sense of humor, it seemed apparent that Jason was once again joining in the family fun.

After Jay's death, Rose found herself at the Atlantic City Casinos more often than she wanted to be. She couldn't stop thinking about her son, and the machines provided a momentary diversion. On several occasions she asked for Jay's help. She remembers one time asking Jay for help, saying, "I know you're probably telling me to just get up off this chair, but here I am. I lost all my money; can you help me out again?" She said to her shock the machine hit $400 and then $500. When she went to the cashier to cash out, she realized that she had an $11 credit. She walked away with $911. Given the amount, she finds it hard to believe it was just a coincidence.

Another time, she felt she needed to win in order to help her family. Once again, she had a request. "Here I am again, Jay. Look down on me. I'm asking you for help," Rose said. "I used three quarters and hit the $10,000 jackpot the first time I tried, and for that one split second, I felt my son with me, and I started to cry. The lady standing next to me said, 'Why are you crying? You hit the jackpot.' 'You have no idea,' I told her. The man who came to give me the money said, 'This machine never hits.'" Rose said that she has stopped spending time at the casino, but she'll never forget when her son came through for her.

Rose turned fifty in December of 2001. Family members told her that Jason had wanted to have a party for her. It was very difficult for her to even think about having a party without her son being there, but she was finally convinced. At the party, they blew up fifty balloons in celebration. Two weeks later, the Christmas tree was up, and the air in the balloons was gone, but one balloon didn't seem to know it. Several family members were present and Rose was upstairs. Somebody came to get her to tell her about the airless balloon that was traveling around the house.

"It went up to the ceiling and it went down; it went to the wall and it was still moving," Rose said. "My little granddaughter started to get scared. 'Why is the balloon doing this?' she asked. 'I think it's Uncle Jay's way of saying he's here, and you don't have to be scared,' I told her. 'I love you, Uncle Jay,' my granddaughter said. Then, it was amazing, the balloon went to a picture we have of Jay with my granddaughter and stayed there. Jay was my granddaughter's godfather, and he really loved her. As we were going to bed, we found the balloon on top of the Christmas tree."

Michele DeFazio, Wife of Jason DeFazio

Wedding photograph of Jason DeFazio; his niece, Alexis; and Michele

When Michele and Jason met, they were both still in high school. Jason, who was always incredibly athletic, was a star football player. Michele, a few years younger and equally athletic, was a cheerleader with a crush on Jay. Their relationship didn't take off until they met again some years later.

Michele was so distraught after her husband's death that it's hard for her to remember all the specific details of the first year or two after 9/11. Nonetheless, she believes that her husband, Jason, often sends signs through electronics. Sometimes her radio will turn off for no reason. When it comes back on, there will be a song that was important in their relationship. Once, for example, she was driving a brand-new car, so she is positive there was nothing wrong with the radio. The radio turned off; when it went back on, the song that was playing was their wedding song—"All My Life" by Linda Ronstadt.

Michele also has a radio in her shower that kept turning off for no reason. Sometimes it also turned on. Michele couldn't understand what was happening. Finally she left it there, but she took out the batteries. She absolutely can't explain how the radio could have then turned on by itself, producing no music but an enormous amount of static. Even more unusual is that she couldn't turn it off. Michele couldn't help but see this as somehow being connected to Jay.

Linda Thorpe, Wife of Rick Thorpe

Like so many of the other victims of 9/11, Rick was an incredible athlete—a football quarterback in high school and captain of his college lacrosse team. From the time he was three years old and started throwing a football, he regarded the number three as his lucky number. It was even on his sports jerseys. When I talked to Linda, one of the first questions she asked me was, "Has anybody talked to you about weird experiences with electricity?"

Linda described her CD/DVD player as an enclosed system inside an armoire, normally set to play DVDs for her daughter. "In order to listen to a CD you have to hit a source select button," Linda told me. "Sometimes we'll walk into the house and the music will start blaring on its own. It's weird. The last time it happened was Halloween, and my daughter, Alexis, was doing her homework; I was reading the paper. The music just started up on its own. 'Where's the cat?' I asked, thinking perhaps the cat had managed to start the CD player. 'She's right here, Mommy,' Alexis said. The song that came on was 'Girls Just Wanna Have Fun.' It's an upbeat song. I opened up the door of the armoire to find the song was on CD #3, song #3. 'It's Daddy, isn't it?'

Alexis said. 'Yes,' I told her. 'I think it's Daddy and he wants us to have fun on Halloween.' We both got up and danced to the music!"

Joyce B.*, Mother of Karen*

Joyce's precious daughter died while working on a project for Marsh & McLennan on 9/11. Nothing in Joyce's background prepared her for any kind of paranormal musings.

"Coming from a background of Judaism, we never talked about questions like 'does the soul survive,'" Joyce said. "I was also the child of parents who had me when they were in their forties. To comfort me, my mother would say, 'After we die, we will all be together.' Even though my mother wasn't a practicing Orthodox Jew, this was very unusual for a Jewish woman to say. I never grew up with the same sense of life after death as my Catholic friends. I remember a close friend saying, 'Joyce, you have to be open or you're not going to receive these signs.'

"I decided to be open," Joyce told me. "What did I have to lose?"

Joyce's decision to "stay open" has had results. Several things have happened in her life that she interprets as "signs" that her daughter is still with her. Joyce vividly remembers the first time she felt Karen's presence. It was soon after 9/11. Joyce, her husband, Neil*, and her daughter, Heidi*, had gone to Karen's apartment to pack up her things. The only two items Joyce was concerned about finding were a pashmina-style wrap that had been given to Karen by her future mother-in-law and a pair of silver earrings that she had given Karen as a gift. From a monetary point of view the earrings weren't worth very much, but they had great sentimental value.

Finding the wrap was easy; the earrings were another story. As they went through the sad task of sorting and folding Karen's belongings, Joyce and Heidi looked through everything. "I finally decided that she was probably wearing the earrings that day," Joyce told me. They left Karen's empty apartment, knowing that a mover was coming to get her things. Joyce and Heidi took home only a few bins. "The bins were sitting in the hall, and it was about ten at night, and we were all kind of tired," she said. "I told Heidi that I wanted to unpack one or two bins, and we sat down on the floor to get started. At one point, Heidi picked up Karen's blue jean jacket to put it away, and as she took it out, I said, 'I really wish I could find those earrings.' Almost on cue, the earrings fell out of the jacket pocket."

It was a very emotional moment. Joyce and Heidi found themselves sharing the same thought. Even though they couldn't explain it rationally, they felt that somehow Karen was there with them. Joyce continues to sense Karen's presence around her.

"I can't explain it," she said, "but I feel her sitting on my shoulder. I know she's there."

Caryn Wiley, Daughter of Mark Rasweiler

Mark Rasweiler worked in the North Tower at Marsh & McLennan. After his death, Caryn was given his car.

"It must have been about November, two months after 9/11, and I'd had sort of a rough day and I came out to the parking lot to sit in the car," Caryn said. "I was just sitting there with the door open. I was very weepy, thinking about my dad and how hard it had been to get to where I was at. I was thinking how hard it was going to be for my family to get through it. The door was open so it wasn't stuffy. I'd been driving the car for a month, so it wasn't like it had been closed up. I had never smelled anything in it before, but all of a sudden it was as if he was sitting next to me. I could smell him. It took me by such a strong hold. I just felt, 'Oh my gosh!' Immediately I stopped crying and I felt comforted, like he was saying, 'It's okay. You're going to get through this. Everything's going to be fine. I'm here and I'm watching over.' I didn't hear anything, but there was this very nice, very strong smell of a person. You know how everybody has a distinct smell. This was my father.

"One time, not that long ago," she continued, "I had my two children down by the water, and two butterflies started flying and weaving around them. My immediate reaction was that it was my father and my brother-in-law, who died in an accident a couple of years ago. My first thought was, 'those two.' It was calming. They

Caryn Wiley and her father, Mark Rasweiler, at Caryn's wedding

were monarch size and two different colors. Another time, my sister had one land on her. She immediately thought of our dad."

Marilyn Bullis, Mother of Dianne Bullis Snyder

Dianne was a flight attendant on American Airlines Flight 11. In April of 2008, Marilyn's other daughter, Elizabeth, came to visit. Elizabeth, who was working in a framing shop, brought a gift for her mother. It was a beautiful lime green framing mat. She thought Marilyn might be able to use it for some of her unframed photos and artwork, but it turned out that nothing Marilyn wanted to frame was the right fit. Both Marilyn and Elizabeth were disappointed, but they put the mat aside. They had a project they wanted to finish.

It had been more than seven years since Dianne had died, and Marilyn was finally ready to sort through the hundreds of letters and cards people had sent. Marilyn and Elizabeth started out by looking through a large bowl of cards that was still sitting on a table in Marilyn's bedroom. They then decided to tackle the cards that filled an antique chest in the kitchen. The chest opened at the top, but there was also a small door at the bottom. Marilyn had not opened this door in a very long time. Tentatively, she put her hand in and fished around. She immediately grabbed something. When she pulled it out, she saw that it was a painting of a flower with a swirling stem. "Look, Elizabeth," Marilyn said, "here's one of your paintings."

"That's not mine" Elizabeth replied. "That's Dianne's. See the initials," she added, pointing to the *DB*. "She did it in high school." Then both of them saw some writing. On the corner of the painting, Dianne had written, "May you look back and smile." Both women felt they had received a message directly from Dianne! Intuitively, Elizabeth took the green mat she had brought and placed it around the painting. Like Cinderella's glass slipper, it was a perfect fit.

A few months later, Marilyn was in a local bookstore. A large coffee table book caught her attention. She flipped through it and let the pages fall open. On one of the pages she noticed a quote she liked so she copied it down. It was part of James Barry's 1904 dedication to his then new book, *Peter Pan*.

> *. . . a safe but sometimes chilly way of recalling the past*
> *is to force open a crammed door.*
> *If you are searching for anything in particular, you don't find it*
> *but something falls out at the back, that is often more interesting.*

Susan Kinney, Sister of Christopher Cramer

Susan Kinney expects that she will never stop missing her brother. Chris, vice president of tax operations for Fiduciary Trust Company International, was a generous, kind-hearted, gregarious guy who was much loved by his family and friends. One of Susan's other brothers, Walter, also worked at the WTC. That day Walter, who was never late for work, was late for work and was spared.

Chris always said that he would die young, but nobody really believed him. Now, Susan wonders how he had this kind of awareness about his future. Susan often has the sense that Chris is still with her and her family. As far as she is concerned, the major sign connecting her to Chris is the number 22. She has no idea why 22 has taken on importance, and she can't recall if the number had any meaning for Chris. What she does know is that after Chris died, the number 22 showed up everywhere. Susan and her husband sold a piece of property they owned, and yes, they got $22,000 for it; she opened a bank account, which included the number 22. She got on a plane, she was in row 22. And it kept happening

Some months after 9/11, Susan and her mother had a reading with a psychic on Staten Island, New York. It was done over the phone. "The number 22 is coming to me, does this mean anything to you or your mom?" the psychic asked.

"Well, it means something to me because the number 22 is following me everywhere," Susan replied.

The psychic then told her, "Well, every time you see the number 22, it's your brother letting you know that he's with you."

Susan has several stories that reflect why she finds this easy to believe. "My brother Mark got tickets to a Bruce Springsteen concert for the whole family," Susan began. "What row were we in? Of course it was 22. I'm not a great sleeper. I wake up a lot of times in the middle of the night. When I look at the clock, it says 2:22. Recently I went to Vegas with a friend. Sure enough, we get to the airport, and what gate are we at? 22. When I saw that, I said, 'OK, Chris, I know you're with me. You're here for the ride and you're going to Vegas with me.' I've been out at a restaurant having lunch with a friend, and we'll start talking about Chris. Sure enough, the check comes to the table, and it's $22. Things like that remind me that he's still a big part of my life. It's comforting for me that I do feel Chris's presence. When I see that number or come across it, it lets me know that he's with me.

"Chris was a big weather buff," Susan continued. "Maybe it's because he was born on December 24th and there was a snowstorm. Anyway, a year after 9/11, they hadn't found any of his actual remains (they were located years later), but the city of New York gave an urn full of ashes from the site to each of the families on the first anniversary. We decided to go down to Key West, a place that Chris loved, to sprinkle 'his' ashes.

"It was a beautiful day, and we chartered a boat to take us out," she continued. "It was an incredible day with no hint of bad weather. But almost as soon as we arrived, it went from being sunny to something like a minihurricane. The wind was so strong, they had to put the flaps down. The power went out, and we all said, 'It's Chris, we know he's here.' As suddenly as the storm blew in, it blew out, and the power came back on. The bartenders rang the bell and said 'a round of drinks for everybody.' If my brother, Chris, had been there, that's what he would do—buy a round of drinks. It felt very eerie, but it felt as though Chris was really there with us."

Chris was a huge Jimmy Buffet fan; Susan and other family members are also reminded of Chris whenever they hear a Buffet song. Her brother Keith got married on December 22, 2001, in Las Vegas. She and her family

Chris Cramer

were all together at the Bellagio Hotel standing near fountains that spray up into the air and sway in time to the music. It was a bittersweet time for the family, and everyone felt Chris's absence. A song was being played with Italian lyrics and they didn't know what it meant. Somebody told them the title was "A Time to Say Good-bye."

Six years later, Susan went back to Las Vegas with some friends. The first song she heard at the hotel was "A Time to Say Good-bye." When the fountain music stopped, Jimmy Buffet's "Margaritaville" came on. Chris would have loved that moment, and it made Susan feel that he was letting her know that he was all right and was there with her.

Deidre K.*, Wife of Craig K.*, a Cantor Fitzgerald Employee

Anyone who has ever been on the receiving end of a "sign" knows how reassuring it can be. It's also interesting that so many people who have asked for signs say that they have miraculously received them.

Deidre told me that many years ago when her daughter Leslie was in a Catholic nursery school, one of the nuns decided to leave the order. She was a lovely woman, and people wanted to help her. Like many others, Deidre sent her a check. The sister responded with a lovely little prayer card with pressed flowers that came from the Holy Land. Deidre loved the card; she framed it and put it on her dresser; it has been there ever since. In 2002, she and Leslie began to visit colleges. This is something that her husband, Craig, would have been very involved with, and Deidre was really missing him. "We were in California, and we were both having a hard time,"

Deirdre's prayer card

she told me. "This was supposed to be Craig's job. I was shaking I was so nervous, and Leslie was depressed. I found myself praying, 'Craig, where are you? I need to know that you're here. Please give me a sign.' I stepped outside of the hotel where we were staying onto a very dirty sidewalk. I was still thinking about Craig. Then I looked down and saw this card by my feet. It was an exact duplicate of the same beautiful card that was in a frame on my dresser. Just seeing it made me feel better. It made me think, 'All right, he's still with us.'"

Deidre picked the card up and put it in her wallet, which is where it now resides.

Maureen Lunder, Mother of Chris Lunder

Ed, Chris, and Maureen Lunder

Maureen remembers walking through a parking lot with her son Chris one day. They both became aware of an abundance of loose change jingling in one of Chris's pockets. Chris surprised his mother by emptying his pockets and throwing the change on the ground. "What are you doing?" his mother asked. "Do you think you are rich?" He smiled. "Somebody is going to find it and feel very lucky today."

"Now I always find coins, often grouped together," Maureen said. "I often find eleven cents—two nickels and a penny or a dime and a penny—in strange places. I find them when I'm thinking or talking about Chris. One day I was talking about Chris and I looked down. There was a dime in the driveway. When I picked it up, the date was 1967. That was the year he was born."

Maureen has had other experiences that make her feel that Chris is still with her. Some of them bring back happy memories. Chris's wedding to the wife he adored was a particularly joyous occasion that Maureen remembers. Sometime before the wedding, Chris approached his mother. "We need to find a song for a mother/son dance," he said. "Because You Loved Me" by Céline Dion became their song. Chris wanted his mother to get used to the emotional song. He told her, "I'm going to play this over and over so you don't start crying."

In June of 2002, a school that Chris attended on Long Island had a memorial in which they were dedicating a tree to Chris. Maureen was driving with her niece to the service, and the car radio was on. "I was wondering to myself," Maureen said. "Will Chris come through today? Will he be with us?" Within the next minute, Maureen heard Céline Dion's singing fill the car—"Because You Loved Me." There is no question in Maureen's mind: This was a sign.

A large number of the men, women, and children who lost loved ones on September 11, 2001, have felt as though their faith was severely tested. None of it made sense. So many good and loving people died. Why? I feel safe in saying that just about everyone who lost someone on that day was confronted with a crisis of faith. I think most of us tried to find a way to maintain a connection to the divine, but it was sometimes difficult. How could we believe in the ebb and flow of God's world in the face of so much inexplicable destruction and loss? The "signs" that many of us have encountered have helped give us hope and a belief in a sense of divine order even while we continue to struggle with our limited human understanding.

CHAPTER EIGHT

Dreams and Visitations

When I started interviewing people for this project, I thought I would be hearing about premonitions, signs, and receiving messages from mediums. I anticipated that people would be talking about the ways in which they "sensed" a presence. I did not expect that so many would tell me about actual visitations. Yet, the first four people I interviewed talked about seeing the spirits of loved ones who died on 9/11. They were all positive that what they had seen was real and that they were wide awake when it happened.

At first I had trouble processing what I was hearing. It's easy to be skeptical about something you've never seen, and personally, I'd never had an experience like this. I was so taken aback that I couldn't resist asking other people I knew if anything similar had ever happened to them. Within a very short time, I had a collection of amazing stories from neighbors and friends.

Soon after I started working on this book, Peter, who lives in my town, told me that when his grandmother died in the middle of the night, he, his brother, and his sister all woke up at that moment, somehow knowing that their grandmother had died. Worth noting is that the siblings lived in Connecticut, Illinois, and California. They all received the message, even though they were in different time zones.

Christopher Carlson, a writer who wrote the wonderful children's book *Puddlejumpers*, told me about visiting a beloved elderly aunt during her final days at a hospice facility.

"I kissed Aunt Agnes as I left for a quick visit to her house," he said. "It didn't appear that she was aware of my leaving. At her home, I sat in her favorite chair, looking out at the two grand oak trees in her front yard. Walking to my car, I turned to take a final look at her house. There, I clearly saw Auntie standing on the threshold, smiling and waving good-bye. I sensed somehow that her spirit was in migration. Before returning, I went to one of her favorite places—the high school field and stadium where she and her husband had spent many happy hours. Again, I felt her presence. Feeling anxious, I returned to the hospice, where the nurse told me that my aunt passed. Thinking about it later, I felt in my heart that Auntie had left the hospice room as her body expired. She traveled with me to her home, and she stood by the door and waved until I was out of sight. Then she walked with me on the field of memories. I shall always remember that hour as a time of great blessing, when Auntie's spirit dwelt with me until her time of departure."

My friend Clare*, a senior executive in a large company, is a practical, conservative woman. She has seen her father several times since his death. She remembers going out to dinner with her two sisters and other family members during the Christmas season following her father's death. Her father just appeared in a corner of the room. He looked at her and others in the group and vanished, but not before returning Clare's loving wave. The most amazing thing about Clare's story is that she was not alone in what she saw. Her younger sister, sitting near her, saw exactly the same thing at exactly the same time.

DESCRIBING THE EXPERIENCE

*Men and women who say they have been visited by loved ones who have
passed on typically describe the experience in much the same way. With
everyone I've spoken to, the visits were unexpected and very brief. A number of people told me about seeing a bright light or aura surrounding their
loved one; several have talked about hearing a sound like a* whoosh *as the
spirit arrives or departs. Most say that although the figure is fully formed
and appears very real, it has a translucent or transparent quality, and
it quickly fades or disappears from view. Typically few or no words are
exchanged. Nonetheless, the viewer usually comes away with the sense
that the person who has passed over has been trying to convey a comforting message along the lines of, "Don't worry. I'm okay. Everything will
be okay." I have not spoken to a single person who talked about a feeling
of fear of the "supernatural" of the kind that is often evoked in Holly-
wood movies. In fact, almost everyone said that once they acknowledged
what was happening, they felt a sense of comfort and happiness. The
vast majority told me that these events left them spiritually enriched and
without a fear of death.*

When Martha*, a neighbor, heard me talking about this project,
she pulled me aside. "Let me tell you, my daughter's godfather died
on 9/11," she said. "But I saw him shortly after that. I walked into
the garage, and he was just standing there. He walked by me with a
whoosh and disappeared." There is no question in Martha's mind about
what she saw.

Gayle Barker saw her brother, who died in the North Tower, seven
years later. She described watching television with her husband, and
out of the corner of her eye, she saw somebody walk from the garage
area into her kitchen. She was more than surprised. "Well, it was my
brother," she said. "He was walking into my kitchen, and he had on a
T-shirt and striped boxer shorts. He was barefoot. He was just walking
by. I guess I believe in these things, but I never have this kind of thing

happen. I'm not one to see something like that. He looked like he always did because that's how he dressed when he was going to bed." Like many people, Gayle wasn't quick to tell anybody about her experience. She finally shared it with her sisters at a family wedding.

Many people told me about experiences in which they felt somebody or something in the bed. Michele DeFazio, whose husband, Jason, died in the North Tower, said that right after 9/11, she was too distraught to be alone. Her sister came and stayed with her. They both started out the night in Michele's bed; her sister was sleeping on Jason's side. But Michele's sister couldn't sleep. She said she felt very warm, as though someone was lying on top of her. She had to get up and move to the couch. Later, the psychic John Edward told Michele that Jason stayed next to her every night.

Arthur and Susan Simon

Susan Simon, who lost both her husband, Arthur Simon, and a son, Kenneth Alan Simon, on 9/11 has never seen either one of them. However, she has felt a presence that she believes was her husband in her bed. She felt him lying next to her, hugging her. She said that it happened at about three or four in the morning, and that she is sure she was awake. "I was lying in bed and I felt a hand on my torso," she said. "It was very real. It was not a dream. I was not in a semicoma. At first it really freaked me out. I wasn't sure if it was my husband, or if someone had broken into my house. I felt a hand, not a touch. A hand!" Susan also said that something else happened on another night that she is also absolutely sure took place. When she was in bed, she felt the dog jump over her body and curl up behind her. Since the dog had died several years earlier, it was difficult to understand. Nonetheless, she is certain it took place.

ASLEEP OR AWAKE

Many have also told me about unique dreams in which the dreamers feel absolutely certain that they have been visited by loved ones who have passed on. Anyone who has ever had one of these dreams knows what I'm describing. They are impossible to forget. People have also told me that they rely on their dreams to help them connect with their loved ones. Before going to sleep, if they have concerns, worries, or questions and need advice, they utter a little prayer asking for help. When they wake up, they often feel as though they have received spiritual guidance.

John "Jake" O'Neil, one of my husband's closest friends, had a series of dreams about Eamon. In each of them, Jake was socializing with a group of people in a bar, restaurant, or party. Eamon would then appear primarily as an onlooker or observer. "He looked wonderful with clear eyes and a beautiful happy smile," Jake said. "He didn't talk or join in. I sensed he was there to make sure I was okay. It was nice for me because he was also able to convey that he was okay and happy. He was almost in a halo, like you would see in a Mass card. He had a certain aura and a sense of peace. I came away with the feeling that he was in the light." Jake thinks these dreams may have occurred at times when he was experiencing some kind of stress and that Eamon, who was always very protective, loyal, and generous with his friends, was there to give him support and reassurance.

Maureen Lunder said that on the night before her July wedding anniversary, she had an extraordinarily vivid dream about receiving dozens and dozens of roses. As she walked through her house, everything was filled with roses. There were roses in the refrigerator and roses in the sink. Beautiful, beautiful roses. Maureen believes that her son, Chris, sent her roses in her dreams to tell her that he remembered the day and wanted her to know that he was with her in spirit

In the first few days after 9/11, Alessandra Benedetti didn't want to be alone; her mother stayed with her. "My mother remembers waking up in the middle of the night and seeing a bright white light come through the window . . . like a ray of light from the windows to my feet, touching my body," Alessandra said. "Right then and there, my mom knew it was Paul and that he wasn't alive. Although she was still praying that Paul had somehow survived, my mom knew in her heart that he was dead."

Vicki Davis, an Episcopal priest in Connecticut, told me about a dream she had about a week or so after 9/11. "In the dream," Vicki began, "I saw all these people who were trying to get through a large set of gates. It was very chaotic, and there was some kind of a jam-up. Suddenly this person I knew emerged from this chaos. It was a man I had dated when we were both living in the Midwest in the 1970s. We had an on-and-off romance and friendship, but we hadn't seen or spoken to each other for many years." She told me that in the dream, she and this old friend exchanged a tender good-bye before she watched him pass through the gates. He seemed to be conveying a message to her that he was safe. She thought it was strange that she would dream about him after all this time and didn't know what it meant. A week or so later, while looking at the *New York Times* stories on people who had died, Vicki recognized her friend's photograph; she realized he had perished. She had no idea that he was working in New York. Vicki, who also has a law degree, told me that she realizes there is no way to verify it in a court of law, but as far as she is concerned, her old friend paid her a visit to tell her he was okay and had made it over to the other side.

Jenette Nelson, Mother of Ann Nelson

Ann Nelson was a thirty-year-old bond broker at Cantor Fitzgerald, working on the 104th floor of the North Tower. She was a loving daughter, sister, and aunt to five nieces and nephews. She left behind dozens of admiring friends and coworkers, a boyfriend who had shared her life for several years, and a 100+ pound Newfoundland named Newman. Ann grew up in Stanley, North Dakota, a town of about 1,200 people where her father, Gary, manages the local bank and her mother, Jenette, teaches art.

Ann and Jenette Nelson

Ann's parents and her friends all emphasize how blessed they were to be a part of Ann's life. They talk about her capacity for spontaneity, unconditional friendship, joy, and just plain fun. Everyone says that when Ann entered a room, it became a brighter place to be. They also talk about how determined, competitive, and goal oriented she was. She liked to win, and it was always best to be on her team. Ann loved sports, just about all sports. Not only did Ann ski competitively, but she also excelled at the pool table. Each summer she would head home to North Dakota so she could water-ski at nearby Lake Metigoske, where her parents have a cabin. She was a strong presence when she was alive; she continues to be so even now that she has passed over. Her parents continue to feel her presence. So do many of her friends.

Until her daughter's death, Jenette Nelson had had no contact with the world of psychics and mediums, but after Ann passed on, one of Jenette's former students told her about a friend of hers named Suzanne Krupp. Suzanne is a psychic/medium in Minnesota, and over time Jenette and Suzanne have developed a relationship. Suzanne has given Jenette messages from Ann that feel very authentic and true. Jenette acknowledges that she was in so much pain following 9/11 that she could feel nothing. For her entire life, Jenette had been the kind of dental patient who always needs Novocain, but after her daughter's death, she was so numb that this was no longer needed for some procedures.

Many times, when Jenette is feeling most despondent, Suzanne, who refused to charge families of 9/11 victims, will unexpectedly call and say, "Ann is here with me and really wants me to connect with you." Jenette is happy to talk to Suzanne. "It wasn't enough for me to know that Ann was in heaven," Jenette told me. "I wanted to know the temperature there." Jenette's visceral sense that her daughter is still around, helping and guiding her, has strengthened her ability to move forward with her life.

Jenette feels Ann most strongly at those times when she needs her the most. In the months after 9/11, as she walked down the hall of her house or the school where she taught, she would often sense that she wasn't alone. Out of the corner of her eye, she felt someone there. The feeling was so strong that she would turn to look.

When we talked together Jenette said, "Before 9/11, if somebody had told me, 'Ann is going to be killed, you will watch her die on television, and you will be speaking at her memorial,' I would have said, that would be impossible. I would be in the hospital under sedation. Yet when we were preparing for Ann's memorial, I found myself writing things down so quickly, it was almost automatic writing. I couldn't stop the writing that was pouring out." Until her daughter's death, Jenette had never even heard the expression "channeling," but as Jenette wrote a eulogy for her daughter, that's how it felt. Ann was there, keeping her focused and helping her find the words.

Jenette has only had one dream in which she felt as though she was actually able to "see" her daughter. In it, Ann was surrounded by a bright almost blinding white light, but Jenette could still recognize her. "Hi, Mom," Ann said. "I'm fine. I'm in the Andes Mountains." When Jenette woke up, she thought about the trip Ann had taken to Peru in the year before 9/11. Ann had loved it there and wanted to go back.

Jenette believes that Ann is sometimes trying to answer her deepest questions. She remembers a particular night, for example. She couldn't sleep and she kept thinking about what it must have been like for Ann during her final moments on earth. The following day the same kind of thoughts took control of Jenette's head. She couldn't stop them. Her granddaughter was with her, and at one point Jenette decided to make the little girl some fresh juice, using a vegetable juicer. Soon after she turned the machine on, suddenly and without warning, it exploded. Parts went everywhere. "In my head, I could hear Ann's voice," Jenette said. "Mom, that's how it was for me." Jenette said that she never heard of a juicer exploding before. I told her that neither had I.

Ann was a strong spirit with an incredibly positive life force. She was also a determined and disciplined athlete, who, from the time she was a toddler, promoted exercise. Jenette laughs as she remembers a cold day when Ann was still a preschooler. Ann went out the door and started running down the road. "Annie, where are you going?" Jenette called after her. "You get back here. It's cold." Ann replied, "I've just got to get my body in shape." Jenette now often hears Ann's voice in her head. At times when she felt as though she didn't have the energy to live, she could hear Ann saying, "Just put one foot in front of the other, Mom. Can you just do that?"

In the weeks right after 9/11, Ann's laptop came back to her parents' home in Stanley where Jenette and Gary put it away. Several years later, Jenette's own computer crashed. For the very first time, Jenette took her daughter's computer out of the closet and turned it on.

She stared at all the icons, clicking first on the one that said "My pictures." There were photographs of Ann and her friends! Then Jenette clicked on GAMES. She had a choice of hearts, solitaire, and free cell. Jenette started to play solitaire, but she quickly realized that she had forgotten how to do it. "Show me, Ann," she thought. She heard Ann's voice in her head. "Just break it down, Mom. You can do it."

When Ann was growing up, Jenette remembered playing more card games with her highly competitive daughter than she could possibly begin to count. Jenette laughed when she thought about a four-year-old Ann wanting to play "gold swish," which is what she called Go Fish.

Jenette quickly developed a routine of playing cards on the computer, with the sense that Ann was with her, but it was quite awhile before Jenette clicked on another icon on the computer. It was called TOP 100. Jenette had assumed this would be a list of music and had ignored it. When Jenette finally clicked on this icon, she was amazed to discover a numbered list of thirty-seven goals that reflected the person Ann wanted to be and some of the things she wanted to accomplish. Ann had not had time to finish her TOP 100.

Many people are familiar with Ann's List because a friend of Ann's showed it to some people, and the *New York Times* did a story about it, as did *Cosmopolitan* and *Guideposts*.

Here, in order, are the first twelve items:

1. Be healthy/healthful.
2. Be a good friend.
3. Keep secrets.
4. Keep in touch with people I love and that love me.
5. Make a quilt.
6. Nepal.
7. Buy a home in North Dakota.
8. Get a graduate degree.
9. Learn a foreign language.
10. Kilimanjaro.

11. Never be ashamed of who I am.
12. Be a person to be proud of.

There are more items on Ann's List. She wanted to "Scuba dive in the Barrier Reef," "Volunteer for a charity," "Helicopter ski with my dad," and "Visit the New York Public Library." She wanted to "Take time for friends," "Be a good listener," and "Remember Birthdays!!!" She wanted to "Kayak," "Drink water," "Learn about wine," "Learn to write," "Spend more time with my family," and "Appreciate money, but don't worship it." Other items on Ann's List include: "Maine," "Knit a sweater," "Learn to cook," "Be informed," "Read every day," "Always keep improving," "Learn about other cultures," "Get my CFA," "Grand Canyon," "Walk exercise but also see the world firsthand." When Jenette looks at the list, she sees Ann's lessons for life, as well as feeling her strong presence.

While Ann was alive, Jenette never wrote poetry. "I think I maybe wrote a jingle as a kid, something about brushing your teeth. I wasn't even interested in poetry, to tell you the truth." But almost in response to what happened to her daughter, Jenette started writing poetry, in rhyme. Jenette isn't sure if Ann is helping her write poetry or if she has angels working with her, but she feels as though she is getting some kind of divine guidance

In November of 2001, Jenette and Gary Nelson visited Ground Zero. While there, Jenette started sobbing uncontrollably, and an iron worker who had been sorting through the rubble approached her. When she got home, Jenette wrote a poem called "Today I Met a Hero." At the end of the poem, she wrote:

I stood there dying-weeping—
As I looked upon her grave.
I stood there dying-weeping—
As her ashes he bent to save
He picked a beam of steel—

He made of it a cross.
He gently placed it in my hands—
As he comforted my loss.
I pinned her picture on his coat.
I clasped him to my breast.
I told him that her name was Ann.
She was our very best.
I wanted somehow to thank him.
But I knew he read my heart.
Just as I knew he was a hero—
From the very start.

Jenette's poems frequently come to her in one sitting. The writing is helping her deal with her feelings about Ann's death. When Jenette has deep or troubling questions, a poem frequently comes into her head that addresses the issue. A major challenge facing Jenette Nelson after 9/11, for example, was finding a way to handle her anger. How could these people have done this? How could they have taken away her daughter? She was angry for herself and she was angry for Ann. She began writing a poem addressed to the terrorists. It's called "Where Is the Honor and the Glory?" Jenette told me that her prevailing emotion when she started writing this was anger. Describing her daughter in the poem, Jenette wrote:

She was small and quite defenseless
She loved people of all lands.
If you had come in peace and honor
She would have gladly shook your hands

As she continued on, she began to see the world as closer to how she believed Ann wanted the world viewed. By the time Jenette finished the poem, her anger was gone. She wrote:

For no man can take our daughter
No man can take our joy
No man will find his honor
As he plunders and destroys
For she will guide our thoughts from heaven
Where she lives with God above
She will guide our thoughts from heaven
Until this earth is filled with love.
For love is where the honor lies
The power and glory too
It will drive away all evil

As sad as she is about Ann's death, Jenette Nelson fervently believes that Ann's spirit visits and helps her cope with life. In a poem called "Life's Plan," Jenette wrote:

For it was written in the beginning
When she and God did write her plan.
For—
To every life there is a purpose—

Ann Nelson and her dog, Newman

For every life there is a plan
That is made with God, the Father,
To refine the souls of man.

Jenette Nelson is not the only person who feels Ann's presence. Paul Murphy, one of Ann's best friends, also thinks of her as an active presence in his life. When Paul and Ann met, she lived and worked in Minneapolis, and he was working on Wall Street. It was a business relationship that evolved into a strong friendship. A memorial service was held for Ann at her alma mater, Carleton College. Paul flew out to deliver a eulogy. While he was there, Paul bought a couple of Carleton College T-shirts. They were in a plastic bag that Paul threw in the corner of his hotel room. That night he woke up to hear rustling and rattling in the bag. It was loud. He got out of bed, tracked down the sound, and looked in the bag. Nothing there but the shirts. "Wow," thought Paul, "that was strange." The following night the same thing happened. The only difference was that this time the rustling bag also woke up his wife, who said, "I think it's a mouse." Once again Paul got out of bed. Once again, the bag was empty except for the shirts. Paul believes that it was Ann giving him and his wife a sign of her presence. There is no other explanation that makes any sense.

Paul is a person of faith; he prays regularly, and Ann stays in his prayers. There are times when he absolutely feels that she is with him. This is not the first time Paul felt the presence of someone who had passed over. He remembers going to a church in Brooklyn with his wife, whose aunt had just died. Both he and his wife suddenly had a shared sensation. They felt energy that they associated with his wife's grandmother pass through them.

After Ann's death, Paul stayed in touch with her parents, Gary and Jenette. Gary comes to New York every year on the anniversary of 9/11; he spends time with Paul and his wife. The Nelsons told Paul that he might want to talk to the psychic medium Suzanne Krupp. Paul called her on his birthday.

"She had some advice for me," he told me. "She said, 'Look for pennies and look for things that are moved on your desk at work. That's Ann's sign that she is looking out for you.' That night my family went out to dinner for my birthday. Out of the blue, my little girl Bridget asks me to hold something. 'What's that, Bridget?' I asked. 'It's my special penny,' she said. I asked her, 'Bridget, why would you want me to hold this?' She answered, 'I just found it now in front of the restaurant, and I think you should have it to hold for me.' It was literally an hour or two after I spoke to the psychic in Minneapolis. After that, pennies pop up in my life in places where they shouldn't be, particularly when I need some support. When a room is clean, like a hotel room that has just been vacuumed, and you know you haven't dropped anything, and suddenly you find a penny, you can't help but notice it. It happens when I'm thinking about Ann."

Paul's sister has had some health problems, and she visited a psychic not long after 9/11. "There's a young woman who has just passed away," the psychic told her. "Her name is Ann, and she's watching over you."

"My sister also finds pennies, lots of times when she's thinking about Ann," Paul told me. "When things are tough, she'll look down and find one in a place where you wouldn't expect it to be."

All this talk about psychics made Paul curious. Even though he said he is skeptical by nature, he too visited a psychic medium named Glenn Dove. Dove was surprised by one of the people who "came through." Dove told Paul that on first readings, family members are more likely to appear, but in this case, there was a friend who was not family. "It's a young woman," Dove said, "and she recently passed tragically. She's sitting with your family even though she is not your family. She's very well accepted by them. She's sitting in the front having a great time."

"I'm lucky," Paul said to me. "I married my best friend, but Ann is another best friend—like a sister."

Another person who has been aware of a special energy surrounding Ann, even after death, is Fred Johnson, who lives in Stanley, North Dakota. Fred has an automobile and machinery parts business in town; he also works with wood and is very skilled at fixing things. In the summer of 2002, the Nelson family put a bench out in front of the bank. It's there for anyone who wants to sit and rest. It has a little brass plaque that reads IN MEMORY OF ANN NICOLE NELSON. Over time, the bench got a little bit bleached and worn out. In the fall of 2005, Gary Nelson took a look at the bench and decided that it needed to be sanded, varnished, and just generally spruced up. He took the bench across the street to Fred Johnson and asked if he could fix it up. Fred said sure and put the bench in a back room, planning to get to it later.

"When I got the bench, I was in no hurry," Fred told me. "I was taking my time. Then one morning, in the late spring of 2006, I woke up, and I couldn't think about anything but the bench. It dominated my thoughts. 'I have to finish that bench,' I thought, 'and I have to do it today.' I had other things to do, but I dropped everything else.

"It was like I was on a mission. I remember that the last thing I had to do was put the brass plaque back in place. When it was attached, I read it out loud: 'In memory of Ann Nicole Nelson.' I said, 'I made it!' The bench was completed. The bank hadn't opened yet, but as soon as it did, I called Judy, Gary's secretary. She asked how much I wanted for the work. I told her I didn't want anything. It was a present. A little while later, she called me back.

"'Do you know what day today is?' she asked. 'No,' I said. She told me it was Ann's birthday. You can imagine how surprised I was."

Ann loved birthdays. Her birthday, May 17th, is also Norwegian Independence Day. Her dad's birthday is May 18th; she and her family always approached these days in mid-May with a great deal of joy. Fred was happy that he'd finished the bench for Ann's birthday. He is a matter-of-fact, down-to-earth kind of person. Nonetheless he views his experience with the bench as special. "There are things we can't explain," he said. "They are just there. I know people have these experiences. As far as the incident with the bench, I feel blessed that I was able to be a part of it."

"In Memory of Ann Nicole Nelson" bench.

All the men and women who shared these experiences with me are successful and stable members of their communities. They are not given to fantasy or delusional thinking. Nobody could accuse them of being in the slightest bit flaky or far-out. Talking to them helped move me further along on my evolutionary path from skeptic to believer.

I admit it; I feel my husband's presence. I think he is with me—not all the time—but once in awhile the feeling is so strong I don't know what to make of it. I think he is watching out for his family and friends. It took me awhile before I could acknowledge this in public because I know how some people react when they hear something like this. It makes them want to say, "Move on. Time has passed. Move on." But I have moved on. I have a full and busy life. I don't spend my days sitting in a corner and mourning. But that doesn't mean that I don't think Eamon is with us. My husband may have died, but our relationship continues. For anyone who knew Eamon and his larger-than-life status, it's not a stretch to think he's in and out of our lives. Many of the people I've interviewed feel the same way about the roles their loved ones continue to play in their lives.

CHAPTER NINE

Mediums: *When Others Hear the Message*

Anyone who has ever lost a loved one unexpectedly and without warning can immediately identify with what 9/11 families experienced. We were all, literally as well as figuratively, in the middle of conversations that would now never be completed. These conversations ranged from the small and seemingly insignificant to the larger and more enduringly disturbing. We wondered why we never asked our loved ones where they put the bank deposit slips or the extra sets of car keys and we wondered why we never learned more about their interior lives and why we never shared more of our own. We were in the middle of making plans for the weekend and firming up vacation travel itineraries; we were getting engaged and talking about pregnancies and adoptions; we were deciding on schools for our children and trying to figure out who to invite to weddings, baby showers, and anniversaries. Our loved ones were gone! We couldn't ask them anything. We wanted to honor their wishes, but in many cases, we had never found out precisely what those wishes were. All contact was abruptly and cruelly cut off. It is no wonder that so many people would have done anything to make contact with their loved ones, even for a brief instant.

Before the end of September 2001, I began to hear stories about 9/11 family members who were visiting mediums and psychics. Several people told me about one medium or another, often in glowing terms. It's impossible to describe the sense of loss I was feeling; but even though at that time I was highly skeptical, I was prepared to take the necessary steps to consult a professional who claimed to possess well-honed skills in talking to the dead.

Mary T. Browne had been recommended by a friend. Nonetheless I remember going back and forth in my mind about whether I should keep the appointment. I was leery and wasn't convinced that anyone had such gifts. When I called to make the appointment, I gave only my first name and no other information. There was absolutely no way she could have known anything about me.

When I walked into Mary's office, I was surprised by how she looked. I guess I expected a frumpy older woman wearing glasses with a slightly spooky persona. Instead, I saw a beautiful, youthful woman wearing a stylish dress.

The first thing she said was, "Someone's sick. Someone's horribly ill."

"My husband," I said.

"He's dead, right? In the World Trade Center," she said.

That she was able to come up with this information didn't surprise me. After all, she lived and worked in downtown Manhattan. I was positive others, like me, had been to see her already.

It must have been apparent that I had an attitude about what she did for a living because it wasn't long before she interrupted her reading to say, "You came to see me because there is something you need to find out. If you are going to be skeptical or angry, then there is no point in your being here."

She asked me if I could relax for a moment and give her and the process a chance, and I said, "Fine."

When she first started talking, it felt very general. Some of what she said made sense, but other things could have applied to just about anybody. And then she got on a roll, and the reading began to ring true.

Finally, she said, "Your husband's name starts with *E*. Is it Emile?"

I answered, "It's Eamon." It was close enough and the pronunciation was so similar that it made me pay attention. She was also able to come up with the name of one of our sons and was quite specific about some of the things that my sons were experiencing in school, telling me that Eamon was paying attention to what was happening in their lives.

She told me that Eamon was a man of superb character, which indeed he was. She told me that he had been bored with his job and wanted to do other things, which was also true. She told me that Eamon was fascinated with the Civil War. This was also true. "He wants you to know that the question he had about Civil War generals was answered," she said. I wasn't sure what his question was, but I knew that Eamon, who was really interested in this subject, probably had many questions.

She told me that Eamon was shocked by what had happened and that he didn't really feel dead, although he had always known that he would die young. She wanted to tell me that he had an easy death. She said he was more concerned with trying to help others than he was with saving himself. This sounded a lot like Eamon. She also said that during the attack, he had been preoccupied with trying to find a way out and that he didn't really suffer. She said that Eamon's mother was on the other side with him. This, I thought, could be a lucky guess.

Then she began to speak about something that totally resonated with me. She said Eamon was greeted on the other side by a man who helped guide him and pull him through. This man's name was John or began with the initial J. She said that Eamon and John or J had been teammates and good friends and were both involved in the same sport.

If you were to stand outside the locker room at Cornell's Schoellkopf Stadium, you would see the memorial friezes of two men—my husband, Eamon, and his close friend and fellow lacrosse player, John Gallagher, who was called Jay. Jay was three years older than Eamon and was a tri-captain of the Cornell "Big Red" team when Eamon arrived in Ithaca. Jay helped ease the way for Eamon, and my husband was always grateful to Jay for acting as his coach and mentor during his early days at Cornell. Eamon had a way of getting into some pretty amusing situations when he was in college, and Jay had been there to help bail him out. The two of them developed a very special and close friendship, which continued after college when they were both assistant lacrosse coaches at Syracuse. In the early 1990s, Jay became seriously ill. Eamon and I were living in the city at the time, and I remember that Eamon tried to visit Jay almost every single day to see if there was anything he needed. I especially remember when Jay complained that he was always cold, and Eamon brought him an Irish sweater. When Jay died in January of 1992, Eamon was devastated.

If there is an afterlife, and if people do get to meet those they care about, there is no question in my mind that Jay would be one of the first souls there to greet Eamon and pull him across to the other side, once again smoothing the way. When I finally left Mary T. Browne's office, I was beginning to change my mind about the role of psychics.

I should point out, however, that not everyone who received a message from a medium or psychic was happy with the experience. Several people told me about meeting psychics who didn't get anything right. Susan Simon, who lost her husband, Arthur, as well as her son, Kenneth, at the WTC, said that the first psychic she saw didn't have a clue about Susan's state of mind. Susan finally said, "I have a broken heart." The psychic said, "He's tall." Susan said, "No, he's short." The psychic went on to say a variety of different things that were not verifiable and were also pretty far-out. The psychic, for example, told Susan that in another life, her husband and son liked to go out in a bang and they were together when Mount Vesuvius blew up. There was little in this reading that Susan found either comforting or helpful.

Susan had a more successful experience when she went to a John Edward taping with Karen, her daughter-in-law. "John Edward pointed at us and said, 'I see a husband and a father.' Karen said, 'It's me.' Edward said, 'But it's not your father.' Karen explained, 'No, it's my father-in-law.' John Edward also told Karen that she was wearing a piece of clothing that had belonged to her husband." Before leaving for the taping, Karen had put one of her husband's shirts on under her own sweater.

LIFE CHANGING COMMUNICATIONS

Several men and women told me that their meetings with psychics or mediums helped them develop a more spiritual perspective. Here are two men for whom this is true.

Alex Ostrovsky*, Father of Natalia*

Alex Ostrovsky and his wife, Genia, immigrated to this country from Russia. Their only child, Natalia, was born in Odessa in 1976. Genia and Alex were very proud of their wonderful and loving daughter. She was a graduate of the Mark Twain School for the Gifted and Talented, Stuyvesant High School, and the State University of New York at Binghamton. Natalia, who was studying for an MBA at Baruch College, had been working at Cantor Fitzgerald for only a week. Alex, a fire warden in his own Brooklyn office, was concerned about the possibility of fire on the high floor where Natalia worked.*

On the morning of 9/11, Alex's wife called to say something terrible had happened at the World Trade Center. All transportation into Manhattan had been shut down, so Alex started walking across the Brooklyn Bridge toward his daughter's office. He had almost reached the Manhattan side, when he saw the South Tower fall. The police would not let him pass. They convinced him to go back to the other side and wait there.

Alex's loss felt unendurable. Then in 2002, he suffered another devastating blow. His wife, Genia, passed away.

At least thirty other Russian families lost children in the WTC, and Alex became friendly with several of these grieving families. Through them, he heard about a medium working in upstate New York who people said was very good and who didn't charge for the readings. Alex absolutely did not believe in after-death communication. In fact, after 9/11, he really didn't believe in much. But he was curious. He was also impressed that the medium didn't charge, because it made him feel that she was more likely to be sincere. From his point of view, there was nothing to lose by making an appointment. The waiting list was very long, and it was almost a year before Alex was able to see her.

To give me some background information on what happened during his session with the medium, Alex told me about a ring that Natalia had purchased for herself and often wore. The stone was diamond cut on white gold and the ring resembled three separate rings fused together on the back side.

"It was very pretty," Alex said.

Alex found the ring in Natalia's apartment after her death. For some reason, she hadn't worn it that day. For a while Natalia's mother wore it on her finger. Then Genia and Alex decided to give the ring to one of Natalia's close friends, Sasha*, who they knew would cherish it.

When it was time for Alex to see the medium, he was very skeptical, so he made sure she knew nothing about him, not even his name. It didn't take long before the woman told him that a young woman, "Na . . . Nat . . . wants to talk to you."

"Natalia," he said.

"Natalia is very happy about what you did with her ring," the medium told him. She also told him that Natalia often visited her friend Sasha and Sasha's two children, one of whom was named after Natalia. "Natalia likes what Sasha did with the photograph," the medium told Alex. Later, when Alex checked with Sasha, who had a photograph of Natalia hanging in her home, he discovered that Sasha had changed the placement of that photograph only a day earlier. "The medium said that she saw a lot of fire around my daughter, but that she didn't suffer," Alex told me. "She also said that my wife and Natalia were together and that Natalia liked what I did with the pillows. The night before, my friend had brought new pillows and pillowcases for my house. I didn't like them and we returned them to the store."

Alex is positive there is no way the medium could have known about the ring; there was no way she could have known about Sasha, her children, or the photograph; and there was absolutely no way she could have known about the pillows in his house. He said he was totally surprised by the specificity of what the medium told him. "It's not like I gave her any information," he explained to me. "I kept quiet and didn't open my mouth." As he left, Alex was thinking, "Maybe there is something to this."

Alex feels that he got some peace of mind from speaking with the medium. He came away feeling that perhaps there was something more after this life. He told me that he is still not sure what he believes, but he believes in this event and the truth of what he heard and how it made him feel. He received some comfort from hearing that Natalia and Genia were together.

Gary Nelson, Father of Ann Nelson

When Gary Nelson lost his beloved daughter Ann, he also lost one of his best buddies and friends. He and Ann had similar interests, and they enjoyed doing things together. As a child, Ann helped her dad with the care and feeding of the cattle at their farm. She was always with him in his pickup truck. That's where she first learned to drive—in the fields and over the pastures. She would sit in his lap and steer the truck. They spent a lot of time in the outdoors; they snow skied; they played pool. One of the things Ann had on her "Top 100" list of things to do in her life was "Helicopter ski with my dad." That's the kind of relationship they shared.

Gary has a solid con-
nection with his faith, but
as he's quick to tell you,
he's also an old-fashioned
Scandinavian guy with a
strong skeptical streak. He
had no experience with
mediums, psychics, or anything vaguely resembling
paranormal experiences.
When his wife began to
talk to Suzanne Krupp, the
medium in Minnesota, he
wasn't fully supportive. But
Gary could see that Jenette
was getting some comfort
from the relationship with

Gary and Ann Nelson

Suzanne, and he couldn't help paying attention to what Suzanne was
saying. He found it difficult to believe that she was so often correct.
How could that be? Gary went through a litany of possibilities in his
head: maybe Suzanne was particularly adept at making lucky guesses
or maybe she was able to piece together information from Ann's
memorial Web site. But Suzanne said many things that she had no way
of knowing, things that nobody had told her and that weren't on any
Web site. Suzanne also refused to take money from 9/11 families and
was definitely not making a profit from talking to the Nelson family.

"The first time I talked to Suzanne on the phone, Ann came in,"
Gary said. "Suzanne was accurate enough that I felt as though I had
to go to Minneapolis to meet her. Suzanne told me things she had no
possible way of knowing. The one message I really remember involved
my brother Glen. I'm not sure whether Suzanne got his name or just
the initial, but she got our relationship, and she described him perfectly. He was wearing boots, Levi's, and a western shirt with snaps

instead of buttons. That's exactly how Glen always dressed. I am one of eleven children; Glen is the only one who dressed in western gear. Suzanne told us Glen and Ann were often together on the other side and they were playing cards. Suzanne had no way of knowing how attached Ann was to her uncle Glen; she especially had no way of knowing that they always played cards together. Every time I spoke to Suzanne, Glen came in with Ann, and in terms of his personality and how he looked, Suzanne nailed him.

"Suzanne said other things that were very credible and very like Ann," he continued. "Suzanne said that Ann wanted to thank us for being so accepting and allowing her to do the things she did. Let me tell you that Ann was a very trustworthy kid, so when she wanted to do something, nine times out of ten, I went along with it. Here's something else Suzanne couldn't have known. She talked about a friend of Ann's who also died on 9/11—a young woman named Amy. We absolutely never mentioned Amy, but Suzanne brought her up. Suzanne said that Amy was there skating on an ice rink to relax. It was an interesting comment. I called up Amy's mom and asked her, 'Did Amy have any hobbies or activities that she preferred?' Her mother said, 'Ice-skating. She liked to ice-skate.' I felt this was one of the strongest messages Suzanne told us."

Suzanne also advised Gary and Jenette to pay attention to birds and butterflies because they often represent messages from the other side. "Soon after she said that," Gary told me, "one of my grandsons was at the house. Now this little boy is a boy's boy. He plays with cars, trucks, and trains. But on this particular day, he headed straight to the Play-Doh and he made yellow butterflies, which he brought to me and Jenette. We kept them.

"At some point, I think it was apparent to Suzanne that even though she got things right, I didn't completely accept where her info was coming from. 'Maybe you should talk to another psychic to see what somebody else says,' Suzanne finally said. She recommended a well-known medium named Char, who has a national reputation.

Suzanne said that she didn't know Char, but that she had read her book and was very impressed with her.

"I made an appointment with Char, and Jenette and I sat down to talk to her by phone in February of 2002. Char told us up front that she identified people who came through from the other side by initials. We told her absolutely nothing about ourselves and only confirmed that the initials were correct. With most of the psychics or mediums we talked to, Ann always came in first. With Char, the first person who came through was Jenette's mother. The second person who appeared was a man who Char identified with the initial *J*. From what she told us about him, it was likely that he was Jenette's father, Johnny. Char seemed to know that Ann was single and had no children. She said that Ann was a very old soul. She also said that Ann was unhappy that we were sad. Char knew that Ann was lost on one of the higher floors of the North Tower and also seemed to know that Ann and I did a lot of things together. Char said that when Ann passed over she was greeted by a woman with the initial *E*. Since my mother's name is Edna, this seemed likely to me.

"Char also talked about a man with the initial *G*, who from her description sounded just like my brother Glen. Like Suzanne, she also told us that Ann was spending time with her uncle. She said they were always together. Char told us that Ann talked about remembering the birthdays of all the kids. We didn't tell Char about Ann's nieces and nephews, but she seemed to know. Char also said that Ann thought Jenette should do more with her art because it was good for her."

Gary was very impressed with Char's accuracy. Nonetheless before they hung up, Gary had another question. "How do I know that this isn't all a matter of luck? Is there anything you can tell me that is more specific that will validate that this is coming from Ann?" At this moment, Char said something so specific that it left Gary dumbstruck. "Ann tells me that you lost the end of one of your fingers on your left hand," Char said. Gary was stunned. Some years earlier, he was in a rodeo and, while roping a steer, had an accident. The end result is that he lost the tip of one of the fingers on his left hand.

"You know I have a hard time believing in another dimension, I don't have the kind of chemistry to have dreams or feel things, so none of this is going to come to me on its own," Gary told me. "But Char really did seem to have some genuine knowledge." Gary's experiences with Suzanne and Char made him much more open to the possibility of after-death communication.

Gary Nelson is a banker, but in his spare time he teaches pool, and in April of 2004, he was in Las Vegas for a weekend pool exhibition and a meeting of pool instructors. The Las Vegas scene doesn't really interest Gary, and by Saturday night he was bored and looking for something to do. From a newspaper, he noticed that one of the hotels had a show featuring a psychic named Dayle Schear. "When I walked into the theater, I went down and sat in the front row," Gary began. "She started out by inviting some people up on the stage, and I watched, but I couldn't really tell very much. When she was finished, she said she would take a couple of questions. My hand shot up, and I got my chance to ask her a question. 'What can you tell me about my Annie?' She looked at me, and I could tell nothing was coming to her. 'Do you have a picture or an article of clothing?' she asked me. I reached into my wallet and pulled out a picture of Ann. I think I handed it to an usher, who handed it to her.

"She held it for a minute and then she asked, 'Has Ann passed over?'

"'Yes,' I told her. I'm pretty sure that I also told her that Ann had died on 9/11.

"'There is a girl mourning her, and her name is Melissa,' Dayle said.

"Well, that floored me. One of Ann's best friends is named Melissa, but what Dayle had no way of knowing is that the snapshot of Ann she was holding had been taken by Melissa.

"Then Dayle asked, 'Where is the big black dog?'

"There was no dog in the photo, but I knew she was asking about

Ann's gigantic black Newfoundland dog, Newman. After Ann's death, Newman had gone back to Chicago with Ann's boyfriend, Eric.

"Dayle had a couple more questions for me. She asked me if Ann was a dancer. Everyone who knew Ann knew how much she loved to dance. She wasn't a professional, but she danced all the time."

After talking to me about his experience in Vegas, Gary suggested that Dayle Schear might be willing to be interviewed for this book. It took Gary a bit of time to track her down, but when he did, she agreed. Dayle said some very interesting things. She said that when she does a reading, she is like a human telephone and she simply repeats the information she receives without questioning what she gets. Dayle is an expert in psychometry. When she holds an object, she is trained to sense or see its history, its past, and often its future. When she held Gary Nelson's photograph of his daughter, for example, she knew certain things about Ann. The name Melissa, the friend who took the photograph of Ann, just came to her. Dayle, who sometimes works on criminal cases, told me that many times she can go to the spot where a person died and get information to help loved ones. She believes that souls come through from the other side and make contact primarily to ease the pain of those left behind. She also believes that a psychic such as herself can go to any location where there has been a violent event or traumatic experience and there will be messages left behind by those who were there. "The messages of 9/11 will never leave that site," she said. "Like a recorder, they will play themselves over and over again. It's a print on the universe, telling the story of what happened to the people there.

Gary was impressed with Dayle's skills, but his history of hearing messages from mediums was not finished. Sometime later, Gary had a conversation with his brother Glen's daughter, Dian, who also had a story to tell. About a week or two after 9/11, Dian, whose career is in public health nursing, visited an alternative health fair about an hour and a half's drive away from where she lives in Northern California. One of the booths in the fair was occupied by a psychic. Dian, who agreed to be interviewed for this book, told me that she had never been to a psychic before. "I had absolutely never done anything like this before, and I don't know why I did it then. Almost the very first thing the psychic said to me was, 'Did someone die recently in your family? I see a young woman and a tragic death. Her name is Ann.'"

The psychic quickly told Dian that Ann was coming through accompanied by Dian's father, Glen. "I don't remember if she was able to identify him by name, but she definitely knew it was my father, and she told me other things about him that were incredibly accurate," she continued. "The psychic said that Ann, who was one of the spiritual caregivers in the family, wanted to make sure that her mother was okay. 'Be sure and take care of Mama,' was what she said. She also told me that Ann and my father were playing cards together. There is no way that this psychic, whom I had never met, could have known that my father was always playing cards."

I was amazed by the messages Gary and Dian received: three separate mediums, totally unconnected to one another, saw Ann and Glen together; two of them saw Glen and Ann playing cards. Gary Nelson acknowledges that his spiritual experiences surrounding Ann's death have altered the way he views the world and the hereafter. "This extra dimension in our lives is so new to me. I've come to accept that there is something there that I don't understand, but it hasn't been easy for me." Then he added, "I try to think of Ann in the present. When someone asks about her, I say, 'She is doing fine' rather than, 'If she was here . . .' Because I know she is always with me." Gary continued, "I am so very grateful that Ann selected us as her parents."

AN AMAZING GIFT

Many 9/11 families believe their loved ones have communicated messages with the help of psychics and mediums with a special gift. Before 9/11, I was incredibly skeptical of anyone who claimed to have this gift. Now, I must acknowledge that I've seen and heard too many examples of some "special" knowledge that defies coincidence. I've talked to several of these people to see if I could get a sense of what they do and how they do it. I discovered that there are no hard-and-fast rules. Some people use numerology, astrology, or even tarot cards as a jumping-off place, almost as a tool to get them started. Some focus on psychometry and prefer to have an object, connected to the energy of the person you are asking about. Some are mediums and, as such, focus on channeling messages from those who have passed over. Some are clairvoyants and are specifically talented at catching glimpses of the future. Some are multitalented and gifted in several areas. I'm using the general term "psychic" to describe all these people. Here are some psychics whose names were often mentioned by 9/11 families.

Mary T. Browne

Mary T. Browne is the psychic I saw soon after 9/11. Mary, who has written several books, said that she discovered her special ability when she was about seven years old and making $.50 an hour doing little "kid" jobs for a great-aunt who owned the funeral parlor in the small Iowa town where she grew up. "I was there before the funeral parlor opened and saw a little bouquet of flowers lift up from the front of a coffin and then go thump down," she said. "Then I saw the shadow of a woman and heard her laugh—a nice laugh, not a sinister laugh—a really sweet, funny laugh like she was doing a trick. The woman disappeared—you know like when you're in the shower and the hot water turns off and there's a bathroom full of steam and all of a sudden the steam goes away. It was like that. When I walked up to the coffin and looked in, I saw the woman I had just seen. And I said, 'Wow.' When I got home, I told my grandmother. She was playing solitaire. I can still hear her flipping the cards down. She said, 'You have a gift. It's no big deal. Don't brag about it. It's okay. You can tell your sister . . . you can tell me. Just don't make a big deal. It's a gift.'"

Mary told me her information comes to her in a very direct way. When a client visits, sometimes almost as soon as she looks at them a thought will cross her head. The thought usually reflects some energy that is current in the person's life. It can be something as simple as the last phone call the client made before coming to see her. Other times, Mary doesn't get anything immediately, and then it's almost as though somebody has turned on a radio; thoughts, words, pictures come to her, and it starts spilling out. Other times, she finds herself talking back and forth with a client to get a clearer image of the issues that person is facing. Mary told me that her complete motivation is how much she can help someone, not how much phenomena she can produce. She said, "The reason to produce phenomena is to help people get faith."

Mary makes a clear distinction between mediums and psychics. She told me that a medium, who is picking up vibrations from the other side, may not necessarily be psychic. She said, "Some mediums are not psychic and some psychics do not connect with the other side." She said that she thinks of herself as a psychic with some mediumistic abilities because she does get messages. She also feels she has spirit guides who work with her. "When people on the other side want to get a message through to their loved ones, they have to give it through somebody who can pick it up," she told me. "A medium is a conduit, and, yes, many times I have been privileged to get a message from someone who has passed over. These messages can give comfort to those who are here." She had bad news, however, for anyone who was hoping to have a whole different set of bigger and better talents after death, saying, "When we pass over, we take our thoughts and our abilities with us. For example, someone who can't sing on this side won't be able to sing on the other side either."

Mary said that 9/11 families sought her out because they needed help getting through the grief and to give them a clearer picture. "They wanted comfort and courage and possibly insight into what happens after you die," she said. Mary emphasized that she believes there is one great God-force and we are all part of that. We bring our experience into this life and we are the highest form of the spirit. She said, "We are the God within. All things pass, but God never changes." Mary then quoted Saint Teresa of Ávila, saying, "Whoever has God lacks nothing."

Glenn Dove

Like most psychics, Glenn Dove discovered that he had a gift when he was a small child. He had his first vision when he was four years old; three years later, at seven, he started having regular encounters with his grandfather, who had recently died. Nonetheless, he didn't plan on becoming a professional psychic; he started out as a musician, touring and recording. No matter what he was doing, however, Glenn always had a real devotion to spirituality and the motivation to reach self-realization or enlightenment.

Glenn, who has been giving readings professionally for about twenty years, lives and works near Rockville Center, Long Island. Since many World Trade Center victims had homes in that area, he has seen a large number of 9/11 families, particularly those related to either firefighters or Cantor Fitzgerald employees. He told me that on his wall, he has a special collection of framed Mass cards from many of the families who came to him. Soon after 9/11, he did a reading for a woman who had lost her husband. She gave Glenn a photograph of her husband, which he put in his top drawer. After that, whenever someone came in who had lost a loved one on that day, he would get an image in his mind of someone pointing to that drawer. That was his cue.

"Most psychics pretty much agree that it's something you hear in your head," he said. "It's basically a thought. It's energy. I'm not really hearing a person; I'm thinking or feeling a person. Sometimes it's an association. For example, when the woman who gave me the photograph of her husband came in, I kept seeing him picking up a picture of my son that was on my desk. It turned out that her son and my son had the same name. Sometimes I see symbols. White flowers, for example, for me usually mean birth or death. For the most part, it's very straightforward. If some psychics hear a dog barking, they might say something like, 'You're coming into money.' I'll ask, 'Did you lose your dog?' Sometimes I will get a fragrance. I once had a woman come in, and the smell of roses was overwhelming. Along with that, I also saw a monk holding flowers. It turns out her boyfriend, who had died, had been a Franciscan monk who left the order to be with her. And it was her birthday.

"On the other side, we have no physical body, no throat, no larynx, no vocal cords," he continued. "So when I say I'm hearing somebody, what I'm getting is a thought projected as energy. I'm thinking the person. Everything in the world vibrates with a certain frequency. On this frequency, here on earth, we have our bodies. On the other side, they have a higher frequency. In this room, there could be a hundred or more conversations going on that we don't hear because everything is happening on different frequencies."

Glenn also told me that when people pass over, they retain the same kind of skills and abilities that they had here. "Somebody may say something like, 'Can you find out from my father what my mother should do about her Alzheimer's?' I always ask them, 'Was your father a doctor or neurologist?' People don't automatically get this kind of information just by dying. They also don't have winning lottery numbers. If I could get information about lottery numbers, then I could change the course of history. That's not how this works."

Glenn sees his work as one of service and helping others and gets great satisfaction by being able to give people in need a sense of comfort as well as a deeper understanding about life and its lessons. He says that he is grateful that his work allows him to help others with their spiritual growth. Glenn, who believes that we've all had many lifetimes, is also a hypnotist and frequently works with people who are interested in past-life regression.

Tom Trotta

Tom Trotta, who is on Long Island as well, has worked with a large number of 9/11 families. He told me that he feels "privileged" to have been able to do so. Tom has known that he had special abilities since he was a child, which is when he first started being aware of people who had passed over. He is an astrologer, a psychic, and a trans-medium. What this means is that he goes into a trans-altered state of consciousness. Images and sounds come to him from his left side. When he sees clients for readings, he typically turns on a fan. The velocity of the fan helps him see and hear messages from the other side. His spirit guides include Saint Thérèse of Lisieux and Padre Pio, one of the Catholic Church's most recent saints. "I want to help people connect to God as they experience God," Tom emphasized, "I believe this transcends all organized religions. I don't think any organized religion has a cornerstone on truth. That is not to say that I'm not a Catholic. I say the rosary every day. My connection is with Christ. But if a Hindu were to come to see me, Krishna would be joining in. My purpose is to help others take those first steps toward a more spiritual walk. If I can help put people in touch with their own faith and help bring them into their own spiritual space, then I feel good about what I do."

Tom firmly believes that it doesn't matter what a person's religious orientation is. He says, "Whatever you are, you can find answers within your own spirit. You won't need psychics or intuitives because you can become your own." In his own life, Tom has had many extraordinary experiences. He remembers a time when his father was in the hospital for over a month; he was in an ICU unit with a feeding tube. "I was crying and praying. I said, 'I don't want to lose my dad,'" Tom recalled. "The Blessed Mother of Fatima appeared and said, 'By tonight I will give you a sign that your father will recover.' That night at about eight o'clock, I was leaving the ICU with my mother and my sister. We got in the elevator and I saw a man running down the hall. On the back of his coat were the words OUR LADY OF FATIMA. I told my mother, 'The Blessed Mother just healed my father.'"

A week or so after I interviewed Tom Trotta, I spoke to Richard, a lawyer who has done business with Trotta in another capacity. Richard told me that Trotta had just made an amazing prediction that had been witnessed by several people. It seems that on the morning of January 15, 2009, Trotta was in the January's Salon in Locust Valley having his hair shampooed when he suddenly announced that he saw a plane going down in New York City on that day. Most of you will remember the details about the plane that successfully landed in the Hudson River on January 15th at about three-thirty in the afternoon.

I called Tom back to find out more. He described the experience: "It was about ten o'clock in the morning, and Missy was washing my hair. She had just started putting on the shampoo, and I opened my eyes and looked up, and I saw a plane going over the skyline, and I said, 'It's coming down. It's a plane,' and she said, 'You're scaring me. Am I in that plane?' I told her, 'No, you're not in it, but it's going down.' So the other woman comes from the back and says, 'You're scaring her,' and I said, 'It's not meant to scare her.' I just saw it in front of my face, like a movie. I knew it was going down over Manhattan. I didn't see it crash into the water, but I saw it coming down. This was about ten-fifteen that morning."

I talked to two people who confirmed what Trotta remembered—the owner of the salon and Missy, the woman who was washing his hair at the time. "I was washing his hair, and he was lying back, and all of a sudden his eyes got very wide," she said. "He was looking at the light that was above. For a minute or two, he was definitely in a trance. He gripped both sides of the chair and was staring, eyes wide open. He made a swooping motion with his hands, like a plane going down, and he said, 'I see it. I see it's a plane, and it's going down over New

York.' He said, 'It's going down,' and he kept making that swooping motion. I assumed he meant that it was going to crash, but that's not what he said. His reactions were so intense it was apparent that he was seeing something and feeling the fear. He also said that he didn't think it had anything to do with terrorism. It was an accident."

Missy said that she has known Trotta since she started working at the salon about four years ago. He has never done anything like this before, although he has told both her and the owner of the salon things about themselves and their families that were incredibly accurate and that he couldn't have known.

Trotta said that when he returned home later that day, his answering machine had several calls from people who were in the salon and heard what he said. "It's very strange with this gift," Trotta said. "I can be looking at a person, and sometimes it happens that I can just read whatever is going on. It's not even a question of tuning in or tuning on to get it. It just happens. I'm in an altered state, and this information just comes to me."

Jeffrey Wands

In the months before 9/11, Jeffrey Wands had a sense that something terrible would be happening at the World Trade Center. He told me that he talked about it on his WLJR Long Island Sunday night radio show. He couldn't be precise about what he saw, but he knew it involved a connection between the WTC, terrorism, and airplanes.

During the few days preceding 9/11, Jeffrey was feeling very uneasy and was having an impossible time sleeping. He experienced the same kind of thing before the 2006 tsunami and the large Italian earthquake. He associates this feeling as having something to do with the large number of souls who were about to pass over.

Jeffrey started having experiences of a psychic nature when he was about four or five. "I remember my great-grandmother, who had been dead for twenty years, appearing to me, communicating that I should tell my mother not to punish me because she did worse things when she was a kid," he told me. "I tried to tell her, but it didn't do any good. I still got in trouble, but it was a great line." Jeffrey also remembers a young friend who he used to go fishing with appearing to him after he died to tell him that he had been hit by a car. By the time he was going to college, Jeffrey discovered that his talent had an added bonus, telling me, "It was a great way to meet girls." Soon it was apparent to him that this was his calling, and he started doing it professionally. Jeffrey said that he has a gentleman, who he refers to as a spirit guide, who had been helping him since he was a kid.

Jeffrey says that he's grown accustomed to having the deceased relatives of new clients congregate before the client arrives. Sometimes he hears them, sometimes he sees them; other times he is given an identifiable image or sound. "I was standing in front of a woman, and I heard the *I Love Lucy* theme," he recalled. It turned out that her mom was a redhead who was named Lucy. Things like this happen to me all the time."

Jeffrey frequently gets random messages no matter where he is. The Christmas after 9/11, he was on vacation at Disney World and standing on line. Suddenly he received a message for the man standing in front of him from his firefighter brother who was lost at the World Trade Center. "I told him, 'Please don't hit me. I'm not crazy, but your brother is standing here and wants to give you a message.' The firefighter brother gave me the name of his ladder company. The brother standing on line pulled out a Mass card and told me, 'I was just thinking about him. Last year we were at Disney together.' Another time, I was on a book tour and sitting next to a woman on a plane. She had lost her nephew on 9/11. The nephew just stood there and said, 'I'm so and so, and please tell my aunt . . .' She loved hearing the message."

Wands finds his talents useful in his own life and talked about losing his precious golden retriever. "She used to wake me up to go outside," he said. "A couple of days after she passed, she came right into my face like she used to do and basically let me know that she was there."

Jeffrey wants to help people bridge the gap and get a greater understanding about life and death. He believes it's really important for those doing his kind of work never to lose sight that they are performing a service with a primary goal of helping people.

I found it interesting that the psychics who spoke to me all referred to the importance of love. "There is nothing but love," Mary T. Browne said. "It is the divine force in action and the motivating factor in the universe." Suzanna Krupp said that without the love connection, she loses the ability to receive messages. She said, "If somebody wants me to get a message from Elvis, for example, I can't do it unless they have a connection to Elvis. It's the love that allows us to communicate with those who have passed on."

"The bond of love is that strong that it continues to exist even without the body," Jeffrey Wands said. "Souls on the other side communicate because they continue to be concerned about the people they've left behind."

PART FOUR

THE MESSAGE IS LOVE

Though I speak in the tongues of men and angels,

    But have not love,

    I have become sounding brass or a tinkling cymbal.

    And if I have prophecy and know all mysteries and all knowledge,

    And if I have all faith so as to remove mountains,

    But have not love, I am nothing.

    And though I bestow all my goods to feed the poor,

    And though I give my body, but have not love, it profits me nothing.

    Love suffers long and is kind; love does not envy; love does not parade itself, is not puffed up; does not behave rudely, does not rejoice in iniquity, but rejoices in the truth; bears all things, believes all things, hopes all things, endures all things.

    Love never fails. But whether there are prophecies, they will fail; whether there are tongues, they will cease; whether there is knowledge, it will vanish away. For we know in part and we prophesy in part. But when that which is perfect has come, then that which is in part will be done away.

    When I was a child, I spoke as a child, I understood as a

child, I thought as a child; but when I became a man, I put away childish things.

For now we see in a mirror, dimly, but then face to face. Now I know in part, but then I shall know just as I also am known. And now abide faith, hope, love, these three; but the greatest of these is love.

—I CORINTHIANS: 13:1–13
NEW TESTAMENT

CHAPTER TEN

Love Is Forever

Getting a message from someone who has passed on is a great blessing. It may not necessarily lessen the sense of loss. It does, however, make you acutely aware that there is more than this lifetime and assures you of love's ability to endure. Time and again, the men and women who have so generously shared their spiritual experiences have reminded me that love is the most important message they've received. Yes, some of them have seen, heard, or sensed the spirits of their departed loved ones. Yes, some of them have received incredible "signs" and assurance; and yes, some of them experienced stunning premonitions. But that's not really what this is all about.

Evelyn Zelmanowitz, Sister-in-Law of Abe Zelmanowitz

One of the many heroes of September 11, 2001, was a man named Abe Zelmanowitz. I heard his story from his sister-in-law, Evelyn Zelmanowitz. When you read about this wonderful man, it seems apparent from his actions in the week before 9/11 that he had some awareness that something might be about to happen, but what's really important is what he did that day in the name of love of God and loving friendship. This is the lesson and the message he leaves behind for the rest of us.

Just about everybody who knew Abe Zelmanowitz realized that he was a good person. They knew that he was a deeply religious man, an

Orthodox Jew, who followed all the precepts of his faith; they knew he was committed to doing G-d's work. They also knew that he was loyal, smart, funny, and generous. His friends and family said Abe would happily give the shirt off his back to anyone who needed it. Abe, who was fifty-five, lived in Brooklyn with his brother Jack, his sister-in-law, Evelyn, and their children. He loved many things—music, *Monday Night Football*, his nieces and nephews, and working with his hands. Abe was a computer programmer for Empire Blue Cross and Blue Shield on the twenty-seventh floor of the North Tower.

Thinking back to the things Abe said and did in the week before 9/11, his family wonders if he had some prescient knowledge of what was coming. On the Sabbath, September 8th, Abe attended a Saturday afternoon lecture at the synagogue. The subject was Kiddush Hashem,

sanctification in the name of G-d. Judaic teachings say that actions that bring respect and honor to G-d are acts of Kiddush Hashem because they glorify G-d and sanctify his name.

"Abe was a very reserved fellow," Abe's sister-in-law, Evelyn, said. "He would never interrupt anybody, but while this lecture was taking place, my brother-in-law suddenly interrupted the speaker and said, 'I don't understand. I know the great rabbis, at the time of the Roman Empire, who were threatened with death if they didn't give up their

Abe Zelmanowitz

beliefs . . . I know they committed acts of Kiddush Hashem. But how is it possible that an ordinary person . . . How can an ordinary person do something like that?'

"And so the rabbi gave him some explanation and continued with the lecture," Evelyn continued. "Then my brother-in-law interrupted him the second time . . . and this was so unlike Abe. Interrupting somebody once wasn't something he did, but to do it twice! But he wasn't quite satisfied with the answer he was given and wanted further explanation. So the rabbi said something else and went on with the lecture. Then Abe interrupted him a third time to ask again. The people who were there say they remembered his questions and were surprised. It wasn't like him to do something like this. It was so out of character. Abe wouldn't interrupt people. He would just sit there and listen. Later the rabbi himself told us about this because he was surprised, too, and he knew him well."

Abe understood the acts of rabbis in the past who took a stand, saying that they would not give up their faith or religion no matter how great the peril. He understood why these were acts of Kiddush Hashem, but what he wanted to know was how could an ordinary person living today commit such an act of selflessness? How could that happen?

On Tuesday, September 11th, just as he did every other day, Abe went to the synagogue to pray early in the morning. "On this day, Abe prayed in the same service as my husband," Evelyn said. "Abe would usually sit at the back of the synagogue; he was really an unpretentious, humble person. And my husband sat at a table in the front of the synagogue. When the prayer service was finished, the two brothers would usually just find each other, shake hands, and wish each other a good day. On this day, they walked toward each other and embraced. Abe hugged his brother very, very hard—very, very tightly. Normally when this kind of thing happens, you don't think about it, but this never, ever happened before—never publicly, never in the synagogue. This is something that we interpreted afterward as his way of saying good-bye."

Other people who worked with Abe were able to get out of the building; they survived. Abe did not leave because he chose to remain with his friend Ed Beyea, who could not get down the stairs. Ed was forty-two years old; he had been a quadriplegic since he had a diving accident when he was in his early twenties. To people who knew him, Ed's good humor and determination were inspirational.

Like Abe, Ed was a computer programmer. He came to work on a chin-operated wheelchair; he was able to type using a stick that was mouth-operated. Abe and Ed were good friends. Abe had helped Ed by building him a unique cigar stand at work; he had helped Ed construct a special tray at home that allowed him to read in bed. Despite the threat of death, Abe didn't want to leave Ed alone.

Abe's family was able to talk to him after the plane hit his building. They told him that there was a fire and that he had to get out, but he told them, no, he wasn't going to leave his friend; he was going to stay with Ed until help came. "Don't worry," he said, "just waiting for some help to get out." Ed was a big man, and he had a very heavy wheel-chair. There was no way they were going to get it out of the building without help.

Ed had an aide, Irma Fuller, who had been with him for many years. She had been on the 43rd floor getting breakfast and was knocked to the ground from the impact of the plane hitting the build-ing. She was able to make her way down the stairs back to the 27th floor where Ed and Abe worked. She found the two men in the stair-well. Irma knew that she could go and look for help since Abe was with Ed. Normally, she would never leave her patient.

"I'm going to get help," she said.

"Yes, okay, you go ahead," Abe replied. "I'll stay."

"Abe was a blessing," Irma told me. "He saved my life." Irma feels she had an angel guiding her out of the building that day.

Abe stayed with his friend so he wouldn't be alone. The two men were ultimately joined by a third hero, New York firefighter Captain William Burke. Captain Burke knew that the South Tower had gone down. He understood the danger and ordered his men to leave the North Tower; he also could have made it out, but he chose to stay behind to help Ed Beyea and Abe Zelmanowitz.

Ed Beyea, Irma Fuller, and Abe Zelmanowitz, at their office in the WTC

Evelyn Zelmanowitz said that after 9/11, her family had a greater understanding of what Kiddush Hashem meant. They have been particularly moved by all the people who have written, telling them how much it has meant to them to hear her brother-in-law's story. She believes it has helped a lot of people "at a time of such unspeakable evil, to hear of such an act of kindness, and caring, and friendship."

People who hear about Abe Zelmanowitz are almost immediately struck by his capacity to love—both God and his fellow man. And people who hear about Captain William Burke can't help but reflect on the compassion and love that he and firefighters everywhere demonstrate in their daily work. The people I've interviewed use the word *love* often in describing their experiences and what they've learned. They say they have been reminded time and again of this most essential lesson of the spirit.

DIVINE SENSE OF LOVE AND PEACE

From my point of view, there are no words strong enough to describe the horror of September 11th, 2001. Even so, in the midst of this gut-wrenching tragedy, some men and women who lost family members have told me of being overcome by remarkable feelings of peace and love. They identify these with great surety as "coming from the other side," often at what must have been the exact moment when their loved ones died. They say that these extraordinary moments transcend anything they have previously known and have given them a glimpse of a divine hereafter. They also say that these spiritual experiences have helped them connect on a deeper level with their own faith or belief system.

Carol Ashley, Mother of Janice Ashley

Carol's talented twenty-five-year-old daughter, Janice, died on one of the top floors of the North Tower. On the morning of 9/11, before she heard anything about what was going on in downtown Manhattan, Carol was at her gym.

Carol and Janice Ashley

"I was swimming in the pool, and as I was swimming, I had a sensation that caused me to stop and stand up in the water," Carol told me. "It was a sensation of peacefulness. It was a sensation that words can't describe. It was very, very beautiful. The place you wanted to be. And it came in a wave—from my head to my toes—and I could feel it leaving, also. I don't know if I spoke out loud, but I could hear myself saying in my head, 'Don't go!' and it went off toward the ceiling to the left. I was facing the west. And I thought, 'I'm going to tell my husband about this. This is really, really something.'"

Later Carol realized that her spiritual experience in the pool occurred about the time that she believes her daughter was killed. It was as if her daughter was sending her a personal message of peace, hope, and love—almost as if her daughter was passing through her, telling her that everything would be all right.

Carol said that she attended a memorial service for another young woman who had been her daughter's friend at work. "Her dad stood up and spoke. He said, 'I'm going to tell you something . . . it's an experience that I've never had before in my life.' And I turned to the woman next to me and said, 'I know what he's going to say.' And he described my experience with the same feelings of peacefulness. The only difference is that with him it happened a few days later."

I found it interesting that Carol had such a clear sense of peacefulness, which she was aware of almost as a separate entity. She could feel it arrive, and she could feel it depart. This was incredibly similar to what I experienced with the wind in my own yard a few days after the tragedy. Unlike Carol, I knew what had happened. When I experienced the wind, I knew immediately that it was connected to Eamon, and I absolutely knew it was his way of saying, "I am gone, but I am still here."

Carol is not the only person in her family to have received a message of love from Janice on 9/11. Carol's other child, a son, was away at college. That morning, as he walked through the dorm, he caught sight of the Towers burning on TV. He knew his older sister worked in one of them, but he couldn't remember which one. Feeling upset as well as helpless, he went up to the roof of the dorm where he lived. That's where he saw his sister. He told his mother that she was "blue" and that he could see through her. He said that Janice told him that she was all right and that she wanted him to have a good life and to do the things she didn't have the chance to do.

Lorraine, Wife of Bill

Lorraine also told me about a very definite and overwhelming sensation she experienced at what must have been the exact moment the plane flew into the World Trade Center.

"On the morning of 9/11, Bill called me at 8:05," she began. "I know that because I was rushing off to work. When the phone rang, I looked at the clock. We had a very pleasant conversation. He said, 'I'll see you tonight.' I said, 'I can't wait . . .' and that was that."

When her husband hung up, Lorraine got into the car to go to her job as a pharmacist, even though she had this strange sensation that she needed to take the day off. Lorraine says that she has a strong work ethic as well as a very demanding job, but that morning, she didn't want to go to work. "I felt like I was five years old," she remembered. "I couldn't help noticing what a beautiful morning it was. I was thinking, 'I can't go to work today. I need to get the dogs and go to the park.' I was like a child who wanted to go play. I was wondering, 'How am I going to function today?' I work in a busy place. I normally look at seven hundred to eight hundred prescriptions a day, and you have to be very focused. So I pulled into the parking garage, which is open air all the way around, and I was looking outside. I said to myself, 'Isn't it brighter in here?' Then I thought, 'It's September. It's the angle of the sun. It's lower. That's all.' And I was still feeling good. But all of a sudden I felt like someone just opened the top of my head and poured—real fast—warm chocolate pudding through my body right down to my toes and my fingertips. I just stopped dead in my tracks. It was completely warm throughout my whole body, and I just stood there, and I was smiling like a silly Cheshire cat. I remember rolling my eyes to the ceiling and saying, 'Thank you, God. What was that for? That was marvelous. You know I'm having a bad day, and you're giving me a little love tap to get me through it.' I was practically floating. It took me a while to realize—maybe weeks later—that what happened to me in the parking lot was at the very same minute when that plane hit that building.

"I don't know who created that feeling within me. I don't know if it was God's touch or my guardian angel giving me a hug of security—like 'hang in there,' or if it was Bill coming through to me for the last time—to say good-bye."

After 9/11, Lorraine had only one dream in which Bill appeared to her but acknowledges it as being a spectacular event in her life. "In my dream I was in my family room and the children and dogs were with me," she told me. "It was snowing—a really heavy snow with big feathery flakes that kind of light the whole house up. The house was all lit up, and I'm thinking, 'Wow, it's from the reflection of those great billowy snowflakes.' All of a sudden we all heard the back door open and close. We were all standing there, thinking about who might be coming into our house in the middle of a snowstorm. We turned our heads toward the kitchen, and who comes walking down the hallway into the kitchen but Bill. We all just stood there in amazement because he looked beautiful; he looked like he was made out of light. Even the dogs, their jaws dropped. He wore a winter jacket that I always favored, and he came over and opened up his arms and pulled all of us toward him and said, 'Look at you, look at you,' and then that was the end of the dream.

"But he was just shining and filled with light, and his voice was making almost a tinkling vibration. It was a high vibration trying to become a low vibration so we could hear him. He seemed to be forcing his voice to be at a vibration we could hear. His voice to me was like magical. None of us could say anything—we were just in shock. Just to see him. Just the way he looked. He looked younger. I remember looking at him, and I knew he was Bill, and I knew he was my husband, but the feelings that I felt at that moment were, *I want what he has!* I had so much love for him then. It wasn't the kind of love that I had for him because I was his wife. It was like a big giant love. It was so big it was bigger than marital love. A bigger love! And I knew at that moment that I couldn't feel what he had inside of him because as a human I couldn't tolerate it. It was too intense. I would have died; it was too electrifying, but I knew I wanted that. And I woke up the next morning and was smiling. I was so happy. I said thank you, thank you for allowing the visit. That was fabulous."

Lorraine reminded me that she had a strong belief in God. "I really believe in the next life," she said. "I know it's going to be fabulous, and I know that it's fabulous for them right now. That's part of what helps me."

THE CARING AND THE LOVE CONTINUE

The overwhelming majority of the people who talked to me say that they are convinced their loved ones are still "there," looking out and caring for them. Further, they believe their ability to feel this presence has helped them move on and live their lives to the fullest.

Jaclyn*, Wife of Carl*

It was very difficult for Jaclyn to continue forward after her husband, Carl, a chief executive at the World Trade Center, died. He was in his office on the eighty-eighth floor of the North Tower. Carl managed to call Jaclyn after the plane struck to say that there had been an explosion, and he had to go help some of the injured.

Jaclyn has many wonderful memories of her husband and the time they spent together. One of the things they really loved doing was taking vacations and trips in the plane that she and Carl, a pilot, had bought. They regularly flew to places like the Hamptons for the weekend, and they also flew across the country, stopping to refuel at regular intervals. Talking to Jaclyn, I could tell how much she loved these trips, with Carl at the controls and Jaclyn perfectly content as his passenger.

When I told Jaclyn about this book, she said that she had a spiritual experience she wanted to share. "When Carl died," she began to tell me, "well, I was the sole owner of the plane. I decided to take flying lessons and eventually earned my own pilot's license. After so many hours of flying, one day my flight instructor told me that he thought I was ready to solo. I was shocked and nervous, but I agreed."

Jaclyn and Carl's airplane

Jaclyn paused for a second before continuing. "We had just flown over to the Hamptons. I was anxious about flying solo, but I put on my head phones, started the engine, and took off."

As Jaclyn spoke, I pictured her behind the throttle—slowly lifting off the ground and becoming airborne—in the cabin flying the plane, all alone. "Normally, on a first solo," she said, "I should have looped around and landed on the same runway. The controller lined me up, but then he suddenly changed his directions. The wind had shifted, and he directed me to land on a different runway. On my second 'touch-and-go,' the controller said a jet was coming in and he wanted me to do a 360 and land behind the jet. This was totally unexpected . . . and something a student pilot on a first solo would not usually be asked to do."

"What happened?" I asked. I could sense the anxiety she must have felt, and I was totally engaged by the drama she experienced.

"Well," she continued, "I suddenly felt this amazing sense of calm. It's hard to explain. It washed over me. I wasn't nervous at all. I was in complete control." As Jaclyn spoke, tears came to her eyes as she remembered the spiritual power and connection that was with her on her first solo flight. "I know that Carl had joined me in the cockpit and was guiding me as I flew the plane," she said. "Together we conquered the challenges and safely landed."

TEACHING US ABOUT LOVE

Many members of the 9/11 community say that the events of that tragic day have given them a greater understanding of the meaning of love. These people have thought a great deal about the love they had, the love they lost, and the love that remains. They have spent time reflecting on the nature of human love, divine love, and unconditional love.

Margaret Arce, Mother of David Arce

Margaret is one of many men and women who told me that the person they lost helped teach them about the meaning of love. Two nights before 9/11, Margaret woke up in the middle of the night, screaming. In her dream, one of her children was being murdered, but she couldn't see which one. Margaret said that she never had a dream like this before. David was a firefighter with Engine Company 33. When the planes struck the WTC, his shift had ended; nonetheless, he quickly responded and jumped on a truck. Margaret remembers David as an unusually loving and caring human being.

"Through his whole life, my son was the kind of person who wore his heart on his sleeve," she told me. "He would stop to help people on the street who needed a meal and animals who needed a home. He was a gentle-man and a gentle man. I think of him as being on loan to us, and it was a privilege to have had him. About a week after 9/11, my son's high school coach came to

David Arce, Engine Company 33

offer condolences. My other son was there and my daughter, and out of nowhere, my dog started to go crazy. The dog just sat by the wall, crying and crying and crying. I couldn't get her away from the wall. She had never before acted this way. Finally the visitor left, and as I walked from the living room to the dining room, I could hear my son's voice. It went past my body. It was like the wind whispering. 'Mom. Don't worry. I'm okay,' he said. I feel as if he is around me all the time and definitely have a sense of his presence."

Soon after 9/11, Margaret visited a psychic, Jeffrey Wands, who quickly told her that she had lost a child—a young man. He was accurate in describing David's personality. Wands said that he could also see a large number of souls in his office who had passed over who were also there for Margaret. David was politely waiting at the back of the room. Margaret, a nurse who has cared for many dying patients, found it easy to believe that there would be a roomful of people who might want to communicate with her. She could also easily see her son patiently waiting his turn. Margaret is sure that David is her guardian angel; in fact, she believes she has many guardian angels. She sees them all as her "precious souls." Margaret is confident that they are together and feels as though she is surrounded by an aura of love.

After David died, Margaret learned that David had a little secret. He was a deeply committed "secret Santa." Cleaning out David's apartment, his family discovered that each year at Christmas David got letters from the post office and tried to fulfill the wishes of a large number of children. He would purchase toys, clothing, and equipment that children wanted and would send it through the mail. He had been doing it for a long time, but he had never mentioned it to her. "That's what David was like," she told me. After 9/11 Margaret and her family started a fund for children in David's memory so that he would be able to be a Secret Santa all year long.

Margaret believes that David helped her understand more about love. She still doesn't understand how 9/11 came to be and how it is possible that anyone could hate so much that they would want to create such destruction, but she knows that David was somebody who tried to bring greater peace and love to the world. She said, "I now know what love is. Love is a gift, a special gift that allows our connection to each other to remain even when someone passes over."

Doris Gronlund, Mother of Linda Gronlund

Doris's daughter Linda was on United Airlines Flight 93. Linda was a woman of many accomplishments. Among other things, she was an environmentalist and a lawyer, with a passion for cars. Linda somehow managed to combine her interests and worked as a manager of environmental compliance for BMW. Linda grew up in Sag Harbor, New York, where her mother still lives. After Linda's death, Doris was comforted and supported by the love she felt from her community.

"On 9/11, my minister immediately arranged a candle-light ceremony at the church," she said. "Afterward, the mayor invited everyone down to the wharf, where the flag was brought to half-mast. It felt as though the whole town came rushing down. There was a field of people. I think more than five hundred people told me they would pray for me. I received more than a thousand pieces of mail and experienced a kind of goodness from people that is beyond belief. My daugh-ter Elsa has also been a rock for

Linda Gronlund

me. I don't think I would be where I am without her support.

"Many friends tried to find a way to create something positive from Linda's life," she continued. "There is a beautiful preserve here in Sag Harbor that we dedicated as the Linda Gronlund Memorial Preserve. People at BMW started a scholarship at MIT for environmental engi-neering in Linda's name. I really believe that whatever we send out, we get back, so I keep trying to send out loving messages."

Linda's last message to her family was one of love. Linda had a strong bond with her sister. She called Elsa's cell phone from her flight and left a message. It said, "Mostly, I just wanted to say I love you . . . and I'm going to miss you . . . and . . . and please give my love to Mom and Dad, and mostly, I just love you, and I wanted to tell you that . . . I don't know if I'm going to get the chance to tell you that again or not. . . ."

A friend of Linda's had an experience the night of 9/11. She was in bed; she thought she was awake. When she told Doris about it, she wasn't sure if she was having a vision or a dream. "Oh, Mrs. Gronlund," she said, "Linda came all dressed in white walking toward me. I went to hug her, and she said, 'Don't touch me. I am all right. I am fine . . . tell everybody I am fine.'"

"Linda's friend thought it might be helpful to me, and, of course, it was," Doris said.

Paul Bellan-Boyer

Paul Bellan-Boyer is a Lutheran deacon who served as a chaplain in the recovery effort with the Red Cross as well as in the office of chief medical examiner.

When I spoke to Paul, I questioned him about his belief in after-death communication. "Well, I'm from Missouri, and you know, Missouri is called the 'show me' state," he said. "Nonetheless . . . these are wonderful events that opened the universe—the cosmos—to our lives, to things that are so good and so real that there is no reason to dismiss them on any basis. Life would be pretty poor if we didn't have these experiences that we could point to and say, 'This whole thing that I'm involved in is bigger and better than expected . . .' I want these promises to be true. Anytime we can touch that in our ordinary experience, that's a wonderful thing!

"My mother died when I was sixteen," Paul said when describing the loving connection that remains even after someone has died. "That was quite a while ago, but that doesn't mean that I no longer have a relationship with her. It's not simply about remembering her as she was. There is still the opportunity for continued dialogue—call it her spirit or her memory as it remains in me. This is the type of thing that most people want to continue and that most people do continue—because the relationship doesn't die even when life ends."

Lisa Bellan-Boyer

Lisa Bellan-Boyer

On the morning of September 11th, Paul's wife, Lisa, went down to the Jersey waterfront. She was able to reach her husband, Paul, who was taking early morning classes at Union Theological Seminary. She learned that Paul, who was a campus chaplain, had walked from 122nd Street down to NYU so that he could keep the campus chapel open that day.

As Lisa stood on the Jersey waterfront watching the billowing smoke, she saw Building 7 collapse and felt numb, thinking about the people who had put their cars in the Park & Ride, who wouldn't be coming home that night. Lisa had an experience that day that she considers a teaching experience; she believes it formative in her time as a chaplain. As she was standing there, overcome by what she was witnessing and what she was feeling, Lisa saw a young Muslim woman talking to friends and pointing to the column of smoke. Lisa told me that she was struck by an urge to go up to her and scream, 'What are you thinking?' But some little voice in my head said, 'Jesus wouldn't want you to do that.' I probably put my hand over my mouth and I kept myself from yelling at her. The next day I showed up at the Javits Center to ask, 'What can I do to help. Please let me help.' The word was already out in the church community that the clergy were becoming overwhelmed, and my husband Paul and I both volunteered." Lisa told me that the very first family she was called in to counsel was Muslim. "I felt it was kind of a pardon for wanting to yell at that woman," she said. "I quickly discovered that many of the workers killed in the Trade Center that day were Muslim." This experience reminded Lisa, who is deeply committed to interfaith work, of the importance of staying true to her core spiritual values.

John Gilbert

John, a business executive in New York City, was one of my husband's closest friends; he and Eamon met at Cornell where they were roommates and housemates.

In January of 2002, John was out with his family in Aspen. He said they all enjoyed a typical day of skiing followed by dinner and then home to bed. That's when he had a dream that, as far as John was concerned, was more visitation than dream. John said that in the dream, he, Eamon, and several other friends started out in New York City, where they visited familiar place after familiar place—jazz clubs, Madison Square Garden, favorite pubs. Every place they went, more friends joined them.

"It was a glorious celebration of brotherhood," John said. "Finally, we all went up to Ithaca and visited all of our favorite haunts there, one after the other. We ended up in front of a bar called the Pine Tavern, but when we peeked in the window, it was no longer the Pine Tavern. Inside a young family was watching TV. We debated going in and ultimately decided that it wasn't appropriate. The celebration was over. It was time to leave. Eamon turned to each of us and gave us a hug. With me, he whispered three words—'Love is light.' Eamon and I always played games together, back and forth, like Ping-Pong, so I had to have a retort. I replied, 'Light is love.' That's when the dream went to black. I woke up and immediately started thinking about what I had just experienced."

John told me that he had so much fun in the dream and had laughed so hard that his stomach muscles still ached from laughing. John said that he had never before (or since) had a dream like this. He felt he had absolutely spent some wonderful hours with his good friend. As he was lying there in bed, a poem came to him. John sincerely believes that Eamon helped with the poem. He wanted to go back to sleep, but he felt that he had to write it down. He was in an unfamiliar rental house, but he found his way out to the kitchen, got a pen and piece of paper, and wrote the poem down.

> *Love is light*
> *Light is love*
> *And as we begin our journey into the light*
> *Let us use our breath as the engine*
> *That takes us inward*
> *Breathing in all the love of the universe*
> *And letting go of all that keeps us*
> *From knowing our true self.*
> *When we meet along the way*
> *Let me always remember*
> *To honor the light in you*
> *And you the light in me*
> *For love is light*
> *And light is love*
> *And this is the force that unites us all.*

Anwaar Ahmed

Just as I was about to finish this book, I received a call from Anwaar Ahmed, a senior executive in a large financial services company in London. He was another of my husband's closest friends. I hadn't spoken to him for about a year.

Anwaar and Eamon met back in the early 1980s when they were working for the same brokerage firm. They were both still in their twenties. Eamon, who was about five years older, was Anwaar's immediate superior at work. Anwaar was born and raised in Italy and married an Italian woman. He currently lives in London with his family. My intense Irish Catholic American husband and Anwaar, an observant Muslim, who I think of as always being calm and precise, had very different backgrounds and very different temperaments. Yet they became extremely close friends. They both worked in New York on the Tokyo desk, covering what was taking place in the Japanese markets some thirteen hours ahead. Hence, they were accustomed to spending time together well through the night and into the early hours of each business day.

"He was unique. . . . When he spoke with someone, he made sure that person was engaged," Anwaar said when describing Eamon. "He was a very passionate person. I experienced my first baseball game with him. I'll never forget working on the Tokyo desk with him. I would be nervous, and he would calm me." When talking about Eamon, Anwaar acknowledged that it is difficult to understand how a volatile personality like Eamon's could also be calming. "His volatility was his passion, and it was how he manifested it," Anwaar said. "His focus was on truth."

Anwaar, who described Eamon as being like his coach, his benefactor, his teacher, his mentor, and his well-being, remembers being with Eamon and listening to Van Morrison music through the night. "If you asked Eamon to explain one line of a song, he could spend hours discussing it," Anwaar said. On this night, it was snowing outside, and just as it started to get light, Eamon suggested that they go outside and photograph objects in the snow, which they did. Sharing his memories, Anwaar said, "Time just runs away from under my feet." Listening to Anwaar, I couldn't help think about how much the poet in Eamon would have loved that line.

Anwaar and Eamon both lost work associates and friends on the Pan Am crash in Lockerbie, Scotland. Anwaar says that his life experiences have made him very aware of the fragility of life. Though he was living in London on 9/11, Anwaar managed to fly to New York for Eamon's memorial service. Given the political climate at the time, this wasn't the easiest task. Anwaar said, "My late father told me, 'Anwaar, you will meet so many people in your life who will like you, but if you can count the people who are true friends, as you define friendship, on the tips of all your fingers you will be a very lucky man.' And he was right. Eamon is always on one of those fingers, and I haven't reached five. The relationship was real. It was genuine. It is eternal. He is still in my life. You know your mother will be your mother even after she dies, after you die. That equation is forever. And Eamon will be Eamon for me and what he meant for me. It's something that I can't articulate, the power and the strength with which he impacted my life."

Talking to Anwaar in 2009, I learned for the first time that he is yet another person who had a visitation from my husband. Anwaar said that it happened about ten days after September 11th. He walked into his darkened bedroom at dusk, and the first thing he noticed was a subtle but distinct odor. "In most Muslim cemeteries, the smell of jasmine and roses and other flowers is very prominent," he explained to me. "That strong smell, primarily of roses, preceded Eamon's actual appearance. I felt immediately that someone might be visiting. Then I saw him. It was his silhouette. He was standing, looking out the window. I was hoping and I was rewarded. How did I know it was Eamon? I just knew. It was him. It wasn't him in the flesh as a human being—just his silhouette.

"In Islam, we have praying beads that are called Tasbeeh," he continued. "Some of them glow in the dark if they have previously been close to light. It's a spiritually soothing feeling—the glow is of a gentle pistachio color, and his silhouette was of that color, so to me it was a visitation. The color was very spiritual, and it was very calming. It was a message of closure. I genuinely felt he was in a better place. Did I need to know that to have closure? Perhaps. But a person who has faith, a person who believes that this existence we have is not 'it'—well, to me, this was another reminder. Eamon was smiling. When I knew him, his lines on his forehead never went away, but this day the lines were gone. It was his eyes, his teeth, his smile. It was Eamon. We didn't have a real conversation. It was a conversation, but without words.

"During this time, I wasn't at all fearful," he described. "As soon as the experience ended, I wanted to make sure I wasn't hallucinating, and then you do get a moment of fear, because it's an unusual experience—one I wasn't prepared for. I turned on the light. The smell was gone and he was gone. That's when I was scared and I was conflicted. I didn't discuss the experience with anyone right away because that was such a profound moment. It was intense. I wanted to live in that moment and not be ridiculed. And then I prayed. I prayed for him. I prayed for his soul, and I prayed to God to forgive him for any mistakes he may have made and that He would take care of him. And I felt very, very fortunate."

I asked Anwaar how he felt the world had been changed by 9/11 and how he had been changed. He answered, "I think we will never solve our problems in the way we always resort to. We talk about different cultures, but you know what culture is: It's what people do when you're not looking. I don't know what we have achieved as a human race from all the 9/11s that we have experienced. 9/11 is a day that represents a tragedy. It's a day with a huge loss of human life. The day has meaning to you and me, but it is much more encompassing than the day that so many innocent victims died. It represents all senseless suffering."

Anwaar told me that 9/11 made him much more aware of our vulnerability. "I attach much less importance to the things I attached importance to before. I am reminded of what really matters in a relationship—what's important when you are growing old. It's not position or title that matter. It's the values that guide us."

Anwaar remembered a day when he came to visit our home in Connecticut back in January of 2001. Eamon was still working on the stone wall that surrounds the back of our house, and Anwaar went out to help him carry rocks. Anwaar remembers one rock in particular. "Eamon and I carried this rock from the side and took it into the back, and Eamon said, 'Anwaar, this is your rock.' There was a hill and a little steepness, and we brought the rock—he and I—down that way and placed it in the center of the wall, kind of hidden. I recall that Eamon wrote something on it. I wish I knew what." Neither man knew they would never see each other again.

Talking to Anwaar reminded me that loved ones who pass on remain with us, simply in a different form. They remain because of love. Love is invisible, but invincible. It's something that we, as humans, will never fully understand. Its mystery is inherent in its power—an unbreakable bond connecting those in this world to those in the next.

I told Anwaar that I would try to find the rock on which Eamon inscribed something and then placed somewhere in the center of the long stone wall that borders our property. How that would be possible I didn't know. Nonetheless, the next day I walked out to the yard and began my search. I didn't find the rock. However, looking out into the yard, I saw, as I always do, the tree on which Eamon had inscribed these words:

Love Is Forever

AFTERWORD

Once in a while in our lives, we are fortunate enough to work on something truly meaningful—something that transcends the spectrum of elements comprising the life experience. For me, this book has been just that—a portal connecting all that is part of one's waking reality to the infinite possibilities of what might lie beyond. Collectively, the compelling stories that are shared throughout the pages of this book have perhaps revealed a few fragments of the answer to the one question that challenges us all, regardless of race or religion or home location—a question that has existed since the beginning of time: What happens to us when we die?

In the end, each of us has a view of the spiritual world that is unique—a combination of beliefs instilled throughout our lives and modified by personal experience. There are believers across a multitude of faith traditions and there are nonbelievers, completely unconvinced that there is anything beyond our earthly existence. "We are born and then we die. That's all there is to it." There are people who go to church every Sunday who openly or secretly are skeptics. There are agnostics and atheists who pray regularly. There are nonbelievers who suddenly find faith at life's darkest moments.

We should all remember that the same God exists across the Christian, Jewish, and Muslim religions; we are all considered "children of Abraham." Behind the religious teachings of each faith, however, throughout the centuries, men have interpreted the will of God differently. For most, their personal mission rests on the belief in a free world with a more collaborative life experience, supporting the individual and, for many, with love as a key driver. But for some, it's the reverse. The central goal is to destroy this paradigm and anything and anyone that serves as an obstacle to personal advancement and power. This is why 9/11 occurred in the first place.

When I started working on this project, I was pretty firmly convinced that the victims of 9/11 were, for the most part, *unusually* good and kind and loving. I must admit that I'm still inclined to hold that view. However, Paul Bellan-Boyer, a Lutheran deacon who served as a chaplain in the recovery effort with the Red Cross as well as in the office of chief medical examiner, quickly let me know that he had a slightly different point of view. "The big thing for me was not at all about how extraordinary these people were, but the fact that they were extraordinary in very ordinary ways," Paul said. "It really, for me, is a testimony more about the essential goodness of people. Again and again, that's what people affirmed. . . . There is a tendency to miss all the extraordinary things that are around us every day in every corner of the world. . . . There were nineteen guys who got on some planes and caused this major destruction, but we had millions of people get out of their routines to help and aid people. I think one of the ways you can look at this is to realize that the violence and the impulse of destruction is truly the exception in our reality. And that the impulse to connect with one another—the intention to practice love and carry goodness—is actually the ordinary atmosphere in which we live most of the time."

When I talked to Paul Bellan-Boyer about the various spiritual experiences of the people I interviewed, he helped me put all of this in a deeper context. "One of the things I hope most people can agree on is that these stories are not signs of pathology," he said. "These are real meaningful experiences that we'd be best not to ignore. And we know there is value in them precisely because they are so important to people and people have relied on them, trusted them, and used them as part of their healing and growth. So even the total rationalist can just take a step back and say, well, whatever is going on here, that's a good thing. They physically didn't use these experiences to go off the deep end, but to go deeper into the reality in which they live."

Paul reminded me that there are things that for most of us are simply unknowable. "The process of making sense is not necessarily an orderly process," he said. "If you've got hold of something that is big enough, you can spend a lifetime making sense of it and make some pretty good progress along the way, but at the end, you're probably still left with something bigger than you can get your mind around." He quoted some of the best-known lines in St. Paul's statements about love. . . . "*For now we see in a mirror, dimly, but then face to face. Now I know in part, but then I shall know just as I also am known.*

"Right now we get bits and pieces that we stitch together as best we can, and the hope is that in a moment of revelation, there is going to be a day when we just kind of get it all, when we will be able to see and live the whole picture," Paul said.

The overall objective of this book has been to share spiritual experiences that occurred surrounding that most tragic day in 2001. Its purpose has been to give people hope—hope that indeed there is "more than this," and that when facing one's own personal losses, there is a place for faith, hope, and love to reside.

A Bend in the Road

For Bonnie

in case i age
    and the strength and
    the fear and the anger
    that i wage is not enough to excite you
in case i go
    and the wind and
    the leaves and the
    sleet and the snow
    don't blow
and the corn and
    the squash and the
    wheat don't sow,
and all things great
    and small
    weak and tall
    don't grow.
in case i die
    and the heart and
    the breath and the
    mind don't shine and
    the arms and the legs
    and the eyes can't find.
and all things unimportant
    seem suddenly sublime
    then the end
    is a bend in the road
    that we'll never find
    a death i will always defend
    you from.

—*Eamon J. McEneaney*

ACKNOWLEDGMENTS

There is an old Chinese proverb: The journey is the reward. This is certainly true of the four years it took to bring *Messages* from concept to reality. It has been an incredible project—truly life changing and, like most books, it took many amazing people to make it happen.

First, I'd like to acknowledge and thank all the men and women who so generously shared their memories and experiences, giving their time to be interviewed for this project. Their wonderful stories demonstrate the infinite range of spiritual possibilities that surround us every day and the eternal, unbreakable bond that only love can create.

Thank you to Julia Coopersmith, whose editing talent and literary expertise served as a beacon and whose friendship I will always treasure. I am forever grateful for her support.

My sincere thanks to Lisa Sharkey, for believing in this project and for leading the effort at William Morrow / HarperCollins, along with Amy Bendell and the rest of the HarperCollins team, including Liate Stehlik, Lynn Grady, Seale Ballenger, Shelby Meizlik, Karen Wolf, and Dale Rohrbaugh.

I'd like to acknowledge the following people for the support they have given me: Catherine Drayton and Pam Bartlett in the early days of the book, Melissa and Eric Thorkilson, Kathy and Peter Skaperdas, Doug Pippitt, John Connolly, Jillian Majlak, Connie FitzGerald, Adele Higgins, Jonathan Levine, Laurie Wulforst, Debbie McEneaney, Tim Guba, Willam F. Lawhead, Dr. Mary Thurlkill, Neil Rosini, and John

McElroy. Laurie Wulforst, Adele Higgins, and John McElroy have been truly inspirational—reminding me how important it is to have faith, and how faith and love together can help a person navigate life's biggest challenges.

I'd like to acknowledge everyone at Voices of September 11th, especially Mary and Frank Fetchet and their amazing staff, for their support and the important work they do on behalf of the 9/11 community.

I'd like to thank Cornell University Athletics, specifically Andy Noel, Jeff Tambroni, and John Webster, for helping to keep Eamon's memory alive at Cornell, as well as Julie Greco and Olena Gutor for their assistance with my lacrosse research. Thanks also to Paul Krome at *Lacrosse Magazine* for his help.

I'd like to thank my wonderful children, Brendan, Jennifer, Kevin, and Kyle, for their patience and support throughout the long period it took to complete this project; my mother, Natalie MacDonald; the rest of my family; and all of my friends for their encouragement and understanding. I love you all.

Lastly, I thank my husband, Eamon, for being part of my life for so many years, for blessing me with our children, and for his help and guidance during the development of this book. I know he was there, behind the scenes, coaching me through the process—as only he could do.

The author wants to recognize the importance of the Voices of September 11th (VOICES) 9/11 Living Memorial project. The 9/11 Living Memorial is an ongoing online tribute that chronicles the lives of the nearly three thousand people lost, and documents the stories of those who survived. By empowering families, survivors, rescue workers, and corporations to create a historical record in their own voice, this extensive collection of photographs, written tributes, and personal keepsakes ensures that future generations will Always Remember. The VOICES 9/11 Living Memorial, currently online at www.voicesof sept11.org, will be a core component of the National September 11 Memorial & Museum at the World Trade Center site (at Ground Zero) in New York City.

Voices of September 11th is committed to supporting the evolving needs of those impacted by the terrorist attacks on September 11th, 2001, at the World Trade Center, the Pentagon, and Shanksville, Pennsylvania.

The author will be making a donation from book proceeds to the Voices of September 11th (VOICES) 9/11 Living Memorial project.

Listed below are some of the psychics and psychic mediums referred to in the book. Listing them in this way does not imply an endorsement by the author or the publisher.

Mary T. Browne
www.marytbrowne.com

Glenn Dove
www.glenndove.com

Suzanne Krupp
www.suzannekrupp.com

Dayle Shear
www.dayleshear.com

Tom Trotta
www.messagesbook.com

Jeffrey Wands
www.jeffreywands.com

Do you have a spiritual story you'd like to share? We'd like to hear it.
Go to www.MessagesBook.com.